# The Log of the *Molly B*

*About the Author*

Pete Hogan is a well known visual artist, who specialises in paintings of cityscape and seascape. Born in Ireland and educated at Cistercian College, Roscrea, Trinity College Dublin and Vancouver College of Art. He has travelled extensively. He is married to Micaela and they have two children, Clara and Joshua.

*The Log of the Molly B* describes his days as a boat bum when he sailed solo around the world by way of Cape Horn in a boat which he built himself. For this voyage he was awarded honorary membership of the Royal St George Yacht Club and the Irish Cruising Club. This is his first book. He illustrated the children's bestseller *Titanic* written by Arthur McKeown

Pete Hogan has exhibited his paintings with many groups and galleries over the years. His work is contained in several public and corporate collections, and countless private collections all over the world. For more information on Pete and his work see www.phogan.com.

# THE LOG OF THE
# MOLLY *B*

Text and Illustrations
by Pete Hogan

The Liffey Press

Published by
The Liffey Press Ltd
Raheny Shopping Centre, Second Floor
Raheny, Dublin 5, Ireland
www.theliffeypress.com

A catalogue record of this book is
available from the British Library.

ISBN 978-1-908308-21-4

Printed in Spain by GraphyCems.

# Contents

# Acknowledgements

I would like to thank all the people who helped *Molly B* and myself on our somewhat tortuous progress as described in this book. Many of you are known to me. Others are completely nameless. From the anonymous fisherman who let me stay tied up to his boat for a night in some windswept harbour, to the passing yachts who gave me an old (and not so old) piece of rope, to the aunties who knitted woolly hats for me and worried about me, I say 'thanks'.

When *Molly B* set out on her final, fateful, voyage, I received considerable sponsorship and assistance from individuals and organizations. In this context I would like to thank Watson and Jameson sail makers, Irish Distillers Ltd., Michael Boyd, Dr Conor OHanlon, Neil Hogan, Liam Canavan and Poolbeg Yacht Club, among many others who helped me on my way. I am sorry that the voyage ended so abruptly.

I would like to thank David Givens and the team at The Liffey Press. The book lay in a bottom drawer for many years until David agreed to take it on. Thanks to Clare Ambrose for help and advice.

To all the people who bought pictures from me over the years I would also like to say thanks. I have had a wonderful life through painting.

I would like to thank Micaela for all her support and encouragement. And for – metaphorically – staying with the ship.

# Glossary of Sailing Terms and Equipment

*Abeam:* At right angles to the hull.

*Aft:* Behind. The back of the boat.

*Beam:* The width of the boat. The side.

*Beat, Beating:* Sailing into the wind. Upwind.

*Block:* Pulley for guiding ropes.

*Bow:* Front of the boat.

*Bulkhead:* A wall or partition in the hull of the boat.

*Chafe:* Wear and tear.

*Chain plate:* Strong attachment points on the hull usually for rigging.

*Chichester, Francis (1901–1972):* English single handed sailor and writer.

*Close Haul:* Sailing up wind.

*Companionway:* The main cabin entrance.

*Dodger:* Piece of canvas providing protection from waves.

*Fetch:* To be able to achieve ones destination when sailing close hauled.

*Forepeak:* Front compartment of the cabin.

*Gaff:* The spar on an old style, four sided, sail which is hauled up the mast. Piece of fishing equipment for landing heavy fish.

*Gaff Jaws:* Y shaped design on gaff to attach it to the mast.

*Gallows:* Strong rest on which boom, gaff and sails are stored.

*Genoa:* A large jib. Large foresail.

*Gunnel:* Solid rail all around the deck of a boat.

*Haulyard/Halyard:* A rope which pulls a sail up a mast.

*Heave to:* Stopping the boat by balancing the rudder against the foresail.

*Hiscock, Eric and Susan:* English cruising couple. Pioneers of small boat cruising.

*Jib:* Fore sail.

*Jibe:* To turn a sailing boat when heading downwind.

*Ketch:* A boat with two masts the forward one of which is the bigger.

*Kicker:* A preventer, usually on a boom.

*Knot:* A nautical mile. Still used because it is the measurement of one minute of latitude. Slightly longer than a mile.

*Knox-Johnston, Robin:* English. First single hander to circumnavigate non stop.

*Lee:* The side of the boat which is sheltered from the wind. In the shadow of.

*Lee shore:* A shore on to which the boat is being blown by the wind.

*Lie ahull:* To take down the sails and let the boat look after itself.

*Log:* The navigator's record of the progress of the boat. A journal.

*Moitessier Bernard (1925–1994):* French sailor and writer.

*O'Brien, Conor (1880–1952):* Irish sailor and writer.

*Port:* The left hand side of a boat when facing forward.

*Pulpit:* Solid guard rail on the front of a boat.

*Reach:* To sail across the wind. The fastest point of sailing.

*Reef:* To reduce the size of a sail.

*Rose, Alex (1908–1991):* English single hander.

*Run:* To sail downwind.

*Sheet:* Rope used to pull in and control a sail.

*Shock Cord:* Elastic rope.

*Slocum, Joshua (1844–1909):* American. First man to sail around the world alone.

*Sloop:* Sailing boat with a single mast.

*Starboard:* Right hand side of a boat when facing forward.

*Tack:* To turn a sailing boat when going up wind.

*Traffrail Log:* Obsolete device for measuring distance.

*Vang:* Rope and pulley used to control a spar.

*VHF:* Short range radio for communication.

| | | |
|---|---|---|
| 1.  Mizzen Sail | 11. Self-steering Vane | 21. Waterline |
| 2.  Main Sail | 12. Cockpit | 22. Prop Aperture |
| 3.  Jib/Genoa Sail | 13. Companionway | 23. Seat Lockers |
| 4.  Gaff | 14. Chimney | 24. Dome |
| 5.  Gaff Jaws | 15. Fore Hatch | 25. Handrail |
| 6.  Main Halyard | 16. Bow Sprit | 26. Anchor |
| 7.  Mizzen Boom | 17. Gunnel | 27. Keel |
| 8.  Main Boom | 18. Chain Plates | 28. Radar Reflector |
| 9.  Reef Points | 19. Tiller | 29. Gallows |
| 10. Forestay | 20. Rudder | |

*This book is dedicated to
Jon and Susie Holcomb*

# 'Go West Young Man'

I quit my job in a paper company in Montreal. I loaded everything I owned into my station wagon and drove west across Canada. I was 26 years old. Boats were on my mind. I was obsessed with them. For some people it is sex, drugs and rock and roll. Some are determined to become famous; others work hard and achieve responsible positions, wealth and a comfortable lifestyle. Others fall by the wayside, get lost in the shuffle. For me it was sailing boats. I had to have one. I had messed about in boats all my life but always in other people's boats. Now I believed the only joy lay in having a boat of my own. I was going to build this boat myself.

To drive across a continent sounds like an adventurous thing. I was in an adventurous frame of mind as I sold up my possessions and made my move. I gave away my business suits and ties. I dumped all my administration manuals in the recycle bin. The West Coast called out to me as it had to countless young men before me. I loaded my tent and my bicycle and my sailing books into my station wagon and bid adieu to La Belle Province of Quebec. What I had gained from three years in Montreal was a smattering of heavily accented French, a failed marriage and the opening balance of a pension plan.

The journey across the prairies of Canada was uneventful. My executive station wagon gobbled up the miles and miles of scrubland.

I picked up several hitchers along the way, slept out under the stars, saw my first bears and endless miles of fields and tundra. The road passes through wonderfully evocative territory, the haunt of natives and trappers not long since. I passed through Sudbury, Sault St. Marie, Thunder Bay, Portage la Prairie, Moose Jaw, Medicine Hat, and Calgary. Then over the Rockies and down the valley of the Frazer River to the frontier city of Vancouver.

I stalked the waterfront and marinas of Vancouver, one of the great ports of the world. The sea and boats are all around, inlets, islands and deltas abound. International cargo ships sit anchored out on English Bay. Logs, escaped from the floating log booms, lie washed up on the clean golden beaches. Around every corner and in every inlet are the tell-tale signs of a boat yard, anchorage or marina – a stand of silver and gold masts indicating the presence of yachts.

I lived in a house in the fashionable Kits district of Vancouver with a bunch of students, ne're-do-wells and lost souls. I sallied forth each day in search of boats and work. Preferably work on boats. I read the notice boards in marinas and yacht clubs. I bought magazines and papers. I cruised the waterfront and back alleys on my bicycle. Wherever I saw the signs of somebody building a boat I stopped and snooped about. I asked questions. I met dreamers and hard workers, people who knew what they were doing and hopeless cases. For the amateur boat building crew is a notorious group of obsessives. A varied bunch of individuals who for various motivations have decided to undertake a project that is more difficult, lengthy and expensive than most of them realise. But they are doing no harm in the main, either to themselves or to others. To want to build a boat and sail away into the sunset had become a common dream of fanatical do-it-your-selfers all over the world by the mid-1970s. I was simply one of them.

I found a job working on boats in the yard of well known Vancouver boat builder and sailor Don Martin. Don designed and built mainly racing boats. It was a small operation employing at most six people, really a custom boat builder, finishing each hull to the buyer's specifications. I had to turn a hand to all aspect of building yachts. I was initially employed as a trainee and the Canadian government paid half of my wages. Don quickly realised I was good at working with wood and was keen and had all the necessary tools. I shortly ended up concentrating on fine interior joinery, which was a good deal for him. But the operation was small enough that I worked on all aspects of boat building at some stage or another. This was just what I wanted – experience as a boat builder and paid to get it. I did fibreglass lay ups, installed bulkheads, fitted through hulls, installed interiors, made the tea, swept the floor, bonded decks to hulls, bolted on keels, ran pipes, wires and errands and came back happily looking for more.

Don Martin was unusual as boat builders go in that he was an Olympic class sailor. An architect by training, he built and designed boats because he loved them. He would take his morning coffee with the workers and discuss progress. Then he would give some orders, jump in his Porsche and rush out to the airport and fly off to sail in the Congressional or Admiral's Cup. He would come back all keen on some new design or technique he had seen.

It was in the middle of winter in Vancouver, the snow all about, on the mountains above the city and on the gardens of Kits. I picked up the local paper and as I usually did, perused the 'boats for sale' section. I found the following ad:

> *Tahiti ketch hull for sale. Fibre glass. 30' double ender*
> *includes plans, rudder and tarpaulin. Located North*
> *Vancouver telephone 12345.*

American yacht designer and writer John Hanna designed the Tahiti ketch in 1930. It is a very well known design. Hanna sold the design to a US how-to magazine called *Mechanix Illustrated* and it appeared in an annual called *How to Build 20 Boats*. The design caught on and became popular. The plans are still available from *Mechanix*

*Illustrated* and possibly at the 1935 price. Hundreds of the sturdy little double enders have been built since then.

All of John Hanna's designs are similar. Heavy, simple, traditional, under-canvassed hulks which give no quarter to the fashions of the time. They have the reputation of being slow boats. 'Total Dogs,' as Don Martin would have said. A True Tahiti ketch should, of course, be built of wood and should conform to Hanna's design exactly. This rarely seems to happen. People chop and change, add and subtract from the simple design, a thing that used to infuriate Hanna. As a consequence, the many bastardised versions of the Tahiti which have been built have given the design a bad name and the words Tahiti ketch are often applied to any double ended cruiser which has a bit of 'character'.

I hopped in my car and followed up on the ad. In North Vancouver under the shadow of the famous Grouse Mountain, in a suburban back yard, tucked neatly under a fine, well built shelter was stashed the hull of a Tahiti ketch, built in fibreglass and far from complete. The owner was a man called Lee Shepard. He had bought the hull from its builder, one Max Hagge, some six years earlier. Lee had brought the hull up the hill to his house. He put it in his back garden, built a shelter over it and there the hull had remained for 6 years while he planned to finish it. He had now changed his mind, had bought a piece of property on an island and decided he did not want to build a boat any more. So he had put the hull up for sale. He did not want a lot of money for it, basically what he had paid for it six years earlier. It just happened to be everything I had in the bank.

So I bought the incomplete hull. It did not take me long to make up my mind. I tried bargaining with Lee but he got a bit annoyed saying he would burn the hull before he would give it away. I found Max Hagge who had built the hull. He was working for a boat builder. He thought it a good deal, but then he would be a bit biased, being proud of his work. He stressed that the hull had been very heavily built. In the end, the shed, in which the hull was located, swung the

deal. I suggested to Lee that, were I to buy the hull I should be allowed to leave it in his shed, in his back yard, and work on it for a period of one year. Lee was agreeable and that is how I came to own the hull of the *Molly B*.

As it turned out, being able to leave the hull in Lee's shed for a year was a big advantage for me financially and practically. A year's free building space was a valuable item, especially for someone who had just arrived in town. Lee even threw in a supply of electricity.

So what had I bought? It looked horrible, a huge bath-shaped object of dirty, slightly translucent, snot-green fibreglass. This was no ordinary fibreglass hull which one sees having come out of a mould. This was a one-off fibreglass boat building project. The hull had been built 'on' a mould not 'in' one. I would later truthfully say to people that when they made the *Molly B* they threw away the mould. But it meant a lot more work for me as the prospective boat builder. A hull which comes out of a mould usually has a gel coat on it which is the colour of the hull of the boat and is smooth and fair. The hull which I was buying had no gel coat but was raw greenie glassy fibreglass. This surface would have to be 'faired' by filling and sanding before it could be painted. Fairing – dusty, tiring and boring – is one of the least pleasurable of the tasks that the boat builder has to undertake. In addition, a moulded hull will usually come out of the mould in the shape and outline to which it will conform to, when the deck is on. The hull which I was buying had no 'sheer' or deck line. While the shape of the hull was correct the hull 'top' had been run wild a few inches above the sheer line and would have to be carefully measured and cut. The sheer line of a boat, the line of the deck at the top of the hull is a very important line in contributing to the look of the boat when it sits in the water. It is a little, perhaps, like certain lines on the female figure. Measuring and cutting the sheer would be an important and difficult operation, which I would have to do.

Otherwise the hull was a strong hull, very heavily laid up. A bit crude perhaps, but to my eyes a thing of beauty. Someone was later to say about it that it seemed to be carved out of fibreglass rather than moulded. That suited me fine.

I cashed in my savings, my severance pay from my Montreal job and my pension plan and paid Lee for the hull. Winter was just coming on and no fibreglassing work could be done in the sub zero temperatures. I must wait until spring. The hull stayed safely in its shed and I went back to my job at Don Martin's boat yard. In my spare time I planned and designed interiors on scraps of paper. I collected bits and pieces of equipment that might come in handy. I bought tools and waited for the spring.

Don Martin was a bit disappointed when I arrived in to work one morning and announced that I had bought a 30-foot hull. I had asked him about getting one of his designs but I don't think he took me that seriously. Now he came over to North Vancouver and looked at what I had bought. 'Well you got it for the value of the materials, which went into it,' was all he could say. Subsequently he was to give me much good advice about the best way to proceed with my boat building project.

Vancouver has a reasonably short winter and it was not long before I could think about starting work on the boat. I decided to call my boat after Molly Bloom, the character in James Joyce's masterpiece *Ulysses*. I had been reading about fellow Irishman Joyce at the time. I have never much enjoyed reading the books Joyce wrote, but I admired Joyce's well-documented struggle and his cantankerous nature. Molly Bloom is probably his most famous female character, the unfaithful wife of the turncoat Jewish Dubliner, Leopold Bloom. A generation earlier her name was unmentionable in Ireland because of the explicit passages in the book which are her thoughts. I changed the name to the shorter *Molly B* form, making it more in the style of names on fishing boats and work boats.

As soon as temperatures would allow the use of fibreglass I commenced work on *Molly B*. The first thing to do was to finish some layup on the inside of the hull. I also got straight down to the fairing of the outside of the hull. This is done by filling the rough fibreglass sanding with a long straight 'fairing board', constantly judging with the eye as to the 'fairness' of the hull. It is a slow, dusty, messy, backbreaking, lung-clogging job. While working on these first basic steps I could plan the more intricate stages leading to the layout of the interior and the building of the deck.

I made a lot of it up as I went along with the building of *Molly B*. But I am good at that. I read books about home boat building. There is an extensive literature on the subject and on the dream of 'sailing away'. I also got advice from my mates at work. The first thing to do, they told me, was to level the hull and have it sitting in the shed, as it will in the water. This makes measurement and fitting easier. A stage of the building tended to be dictated by the foregoing one. It was like some sort of a giant jigsaw puzzle. It was not a matter of

reading the instructions. There were none. This was not a series of mouldings which fitted together in kit form to produce a boat. I had a rough hull and had to figure out the rest.

First I installed a floor in the hull which gave me something to stand on rather than scramble about in the huge empty hull moulding. I bought vast quantities of plywood. Good thick locally made plywood, probably the best in the world. The bulkheads went in next. I started with the main bulkhead and the strategically important ones at either end of the cabin. I had the interior layout sketched out using Hanna's plans as a starting point and adhered to a time-honoured simple layout common on many small boats. This involves a seat bunk located on either side of the cabin, a galley to port below the companionway and a navigation area to starboard. In the forepeak and aft was storage, lots of storage. If I had been an architect, as I had once wanted to, I think I would have been a modernist. People in those days talked about stripped out racing boats. *Molly B* was a sort of stripped out cruising boat. Perhaps the most unusual thing about the design would be the list of things that the boat did not have. No motor of course, just a huge storage area where the motor should have been. No toilet or shower, electrics or electronics. Bucket and chuck it.

Bulkheads are the walls in a boat, providing stiffness to the hull and the modules onto which to build the rest of the interior. Every place in the hull where something is going to happen – a bunk, a locker, a galley, a seat, a chainplate or stress point – must first have a bulkhead or two in place. There were many of them. I became a dab hand at measuring them out, taking offsets with level, square and measuring tape, then cutting them out with a jigsaw and bonding them in against the curve of the hull.

From my work with Don Martin I knew that it was best to do as much work inside the hull before building the deck. This I did, roughing out the interior. I built bunks, lockers and the galley. I moulded in place two huge water tanks. Then it was time to build on the decks and cabin profile.

I retained the simple cabin proportions designed by Hanna with  its boxy shape and wide side decks. The deck was of the local plywood and the interior trim of the beautiful local red cedar. I overbuilt it a little but better to overbuild a cruising boat than to underbuild it I thought. I covered the plywood deck with a layer of epoxy fibreglass on Don Martin's advice.

I still had to cut the sheer line, an important aesthetic aspect of a yacht. I measured carefully from the plans. Then I measured again. I tried to eyeball it from outside the shed. Then I measured it again. Then I got out my skill saw and cut the thing. I built a cap rail and rubbing strip out of fibreglass, copying what would have been wood in the plans. Finally I insulated the interior with a layer of foam covered in fibreglass.

There were other details which I worked on concurrently. The transom hung rudder, some clever seat lockers, the fore hatch; all came together in an orgy of fibreglassing. It was a long dedicated summer as I worked away alone in the back garden above Burrard inlet.

Come the autumn it was time to move *Molly B*. It was part of the agreement with Lee who had sold me the hull. I found a wonderful shed in the False Creek area of Vancouver which was being used by a group of boat builders and dreamers. The building had been a light engineering works in a previous existence and still had its overhead gantry crane. I rented a corner, moved *Molly B* one snowy fall Saturday morning, and built a barricade of salvaged hoarding around her. I moved all my tools and books in alongside, gave up my rented shared house and moved in to the unfinished *Molly B*. As snug as a clam in a mud bank.

There I stayed for a further two years. I slowly finished the detail of the boat when the mood took me. I wrote off to the famous Lunenburg foundry in Nova Scotia and ordered a nifty little wood burning stove. I installed a good bilge pump, the rudder, hand rails, cleats, winches, anchor bits and chainplates. I cut portholes in the cabin sides I built a bow sprit, tiller, booms and a gaff. I drove up into the hinterland of British Columbia with a friend and cut down two trees to use as masts. We shipped them down to the city on a huge station wagon. I sent off to Hong Kong for a set of sails.

Bernard Moitessier had been keen on interior steering positions and a craze for Perspex domes on salty cruising boats had developed. My buddy Patrick and I found a supply of Perspex domes on the roof of newspaper selling kiosks stored in the parking lot of the Vancouver Sun. One dark night, with the help of an adjustable wrench, that's how *Molly B* got her Perspex dome. I never got around to building the interior steering wheel, but the Moitessier dome let in a lot of light on to the chart table.

I did a lot of salvaging and improvising. A logical trick when I needed something was to go and check out the skips at the back of marine stores or boat builders. It's amazing what they were throwing out.

I might still be there in that comfy wooden shed on the slopes above False Creek. I was enjoying life living in my boat on safe dry land. But the shed was more valuable to the property developers who owned it. They wanted to turn it into townhouses. The boat builders and their dreams were given their walking papers. On a cold November Saturday morning I launched *Molly B* into Burrard inlet. A friend's wife christened her with a bottle of fizzy BC apple juice. Patrick in *Sunar*, his converted lifeboat, towed *Molly B* to its first anchorage. We all gathered round and were able to step the mast by hand while the boat was at anchor in False Creek.

## 2

# 'A Poor Wayfaring Stranger'

*'I'm just a poor wayfaring stranger
Travelling through this land of woe'*

I lived on board the boat from the first day that it was launched. *Molly B* was anchored in False Creek, the calm inlet that fringes the south side of the peninsula that is Vancouver City. False Creek and the land around it, Grandville Island and the slopes above the creek were undergoing rapid gentrification. It had been a rinky dink industrial area, now it was becoming a highly desirable residential one. *Molly B* was parked with a small group of other yachts, appropriately enough, on the site of a proposed marina. Every now and again each of the boats would get letters from the city manager telling them to move on or else. I used the letters to light the fire in the wood burning stove. Winter was rapidly closing in.

Ernest lived nearby. He would call by in his own boat delivering a load of firewood and some books about voyaging. Ernest had wanted to do what I was going to do – sail away in a boat he would build himself. But instead he had married and found religion. He would come by at night when his kids had been tucked into bed and play the guitar. One song he wrote in the log:

*I'm just a poor wayfaring stranger*
*Travelling through this land of woe*
*And there's no sickness toil or danger*
*In this bright land to which I go*
*I'm going back to see my sister*
*I'm going back no more to roam*
*I'm just a travelling over Jordan*
*I'm just a travelling over home.*

Living on board a boat in a well-protected anchorage in winter with the snow on deck is a surprisingly pleasant existence. There is no incentive to go anywhere. No feeling of guilt that the boat is not being used for the purposes for which it was built. If there is a good stove, a plentiful supply of firewood, a tarp over the boom, some interesting books and a good sleeping bag then life is complete.

I spliced and fitted the rigging of *Molly B* while the boat was in the water and the masts standing. This was not an easy thing to do. It is a job which involves much climbing of the masts and juggling of temporary stays. I used cheap galvanised wire called guy line wire

of a type which was much used by the fishermen. It was designed for the staying of telephone poles. It had seven very thick strands but was surprisingly easy to splice using a wrap around technique rather than a tuck under, proper marine technique. All that was needed to make the splice was a vicegrips and a tough pair of hands.

The gaff rig requires a vast amount of rope, much more than the conventional Bermudan rig. Apart from the usual halyards and sheets, some of them going up and down the mast many times, there are uphauls, downhauls, outhauls, preventers, guys and pennants. Not to mention the mess of anchor lines, shore lines and spare lines. Things were tied on, lashed or whipped rather than secured with patent, stainless steel yacht fittings. *Molly B* was a ropey boat in more ways than one. Then care has to be taken that the rope does not chaff on other parts of the boat or on itself or on the rigging. To work the rope a huge number of blocks of all types are required.

By February the snow had cleared off the deck and off the slopes of the mountains behind Vancouver. The rigging was in place and the sails bent on. I was anxious to take *Molly B* out for a first sail. I

squeezed and bumped and rowed the engineless *Molly B* out through the narrow entrance and the swing rail bridge guarding False Creek, anchoring in the shadow of the Jericho Hangars at English Bay.

Joss came along for a trial sail – a sort of a shake down cruise. Coming from the plains of Saskatchewan as he did, he knew nothing about sailing. But he was keen to try a bit of fishing. Boats for Joss were a platform from which to fish. We set sail for the islands to the north of Vancouver. Things were going well till we hit a squall just north of Bowen Island. This is at the entrance to Howe Sound, one of the most majestic fjords on the Pacific Northwest coast. *Molly B* heeled over in the gust. The hull surged forward in the flat sea. Every piece of rope and rigging strained. Suddenly the main mast canted over at an odd angle, the new unstretched rigging unable to hold it. CRACK! The main mast broke in two about half way up its length and the whole rig – mast, gaff, mainsail and genoa – disappeared over the port bow into the sea. So much for a shake down cruise.

I lost my cool. I ran around shouting incomprehensible orders at Joss. I pulled ropes and grabbed tools, cursed and swore. Joss thought that this was a normal occurrence for those who go sailing. 'Now I wonder,' he said, 'would this be a good place for a spot of fishing?'

We drifted up the sound, out of control but in no danger. The squall passed and we hauled the mess of rigging, sails and broken spar aboard. The mizzen mast was still standing but was located so far aft that *Molly B* would not sail under such an unbalanced rig. The boat was hove to and would not respond to the tiller. I sent Joss up to the bow with the huge sculling oar and we succeeded in making progress by counterbalancing the turning moment of the mizzen with the oar at the bow. In this way, sailing down wind, we made the nearby fishing village of Gibsons in time for a beer and pizza dinner.

Gibsons is surrounded by trees. It must be the one thing they have a surplus of. So next day we went out and cut down another one a short distance from the town. Joss is a handy man to have around for this sort of activity. He knows the local customs and how far one can go without offending the local sensibilities. Not to mention the law. We were lucky also in getting transportation for our new mast down to the harbour, in effect hitching a lift from a truck and asking if we could bring our tree along with us. Friendly people in Gibsons.

There were dredging operations under way in Gibsons' harbour. This made it uncomfortable for both living on board and building new masts. The noisy dredging barge was less than 20 meters away and threw up a tidal wave each time it plonked its bucket into the harbour. Joss had to depart. He had a job to get back to in Vancouver and hitched a lift on a boat being delivered there. He went off smiling but apologising as he felt that he was leaving me in the lurch. He wanted to see the adventure out. He was soon replaced. Who should I then run into but Jennifer and her boyfriend Goof?

They were living nearby and building a dugout canoe. Goof knew the area well and advised me to take my tree over to Plumper Cove about a mile from Gibsons. There was a picnic jetty there and I would be able to build my mast in peace.

Getting to Plumper Cove without Joss on the oar was not easy. Luckily there was little or no wind the following morning – a misty, cold, calm, Pacific Northwest day. I got an early start so that no one would witness the spectacle. I loaded my newly cut tree on top of the cabin and lashed the tiller of *Molly B*. I then clambered into the dinghy, cast off and rowed the 6-ton *Molly B* the mile across the inlet to Plumper Cove. There I tied up in the empty, out of season, picnic area, brought the mast ashore and set to work.

Two days of adzing, sawing, planing and fitting and the new mast was ready to be stepped. The mast of a traditionally rigged small boat is a very simple piece of equipment, almost like a giant toothpick. To avoid repetition of the recent accident I moved the mainmast chainplates aft a bit to give them a better angle of support. I also made a resolution to fit running backstays to add extra support even though the design did not call for them.

Goof and Jennifer arrived over from Gibsons in time to help me with the stepping of the new mast. To do this I beached *Molly B* on the top of the tide, leaning the hull against the jetty at Plumper Cove. Goof and myself were then able to lower the new mast into position from the top of the pier. A further day of adjusting and fitting and rigging and the boat was ready to go sailing. Not bad for an emergency running repair. Four days of work at Plumper Cove and a week after the initial dismasting and *Molly B* was better than new.

Jennifer and Goof stayed for another day and we went for a short sail on Goof's boat. Called the *Pukmis*, it was a cross between a dhow and a schooner. Goof had built it himself. He said that he had found

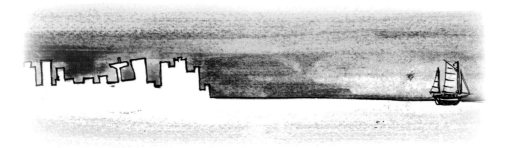

a log floating in Georgia Straight. He towed the log to a sawmill, had it milled into lumber and then had built *Pukmis* on a beach using drawings out of various library books as his inspiration for the design. You can do that sort of thing in the bays and inlets of the Gulf.

Then the two of them sailed away from Plumper Cove and I don't think I ever saw them again. *Molly B* set sail for Vancouver. The shake down cruise was over. I had a big list of things to do, change, get or make, but the cruise proper could now begin. I would fix things as I went along.

The autumn is the recommended season for yachts to head out from Vancouver and the Pacific Northwest and go south. Now it was early March. I was in a hurry. I had somehow convinced myself that if I could quickly get down to the Panama Canal and through it, I would be able to sail across the Atlantic that same summer. This is the sort of hopelessly ambitious plan which comes of gazing at world maps. But there was nothing holding me in Vancouver. I had sold my car, packed all my tools on board the boat and given away what few possessions I had. All of a sudden I was 'a man in a hurry'. I wanted to be on my way.

Joss volunteered to come along for the first hop, as far as Victoria. He was taking to this yachting lark. We used his truck for last minute messages and then on a Monday morning in March, *Molly B* departed Vancouver, outward bound for Ireland. By evening as the light faded we were three miles from our starting point, anchored against a strong tide in calm weather on the banks of the Fraser River delta. We played a game of chess. Joss is never happier than when playing chess. He claimed to have been a child prodigy at the game. I never came close to beating him and he never tired of playing. 'No, no, don't do that!' was his most common retort. And he would let me make a new move.

Night was coming on and with it a bit of a breeze from the northwest. We upped anchor and beat across English bay to the tiny Caulfield Cove. We spent a snug night in the small cove and got a rainy,

wet, late start the next day. Then our luck, and the wind, changed. We headed out across the 25 miles of the Georgia Strait in a steady west wind with bad visibility from the misty low clouds. Aiming to pass north of the 13-mile long Galiano Island, night had fallen by the time *Molly B* closed with the shore. Joss, up on the bow, saw the surf line first and we jibed and ran down the length of Galiano. I had gauged the currents wrong when crossing the strait and we were too far to the south. We would have to go through Active Pass with its 8-knot currents. As its name implies, Active Pass is a busy junction on the Vancouver/Victoria ferry route. With its strong currents, ferry traffic and off lying shoals, Active Pass is nowhere to be messing about, at night, in an engineless boat. More by luck than anything else we arrived at slack water, the period in between tides. I was also able to follow a barge heading in towards the pass as a guide. I consulted my charts and decided that discretion might not be out of place. *Molly B* nipped into the convenient little ferry terminal of Sturdies Bay, which is on the Vancouver side of the pass. There we did a neat job of tying up for the night at a water taxi terminal. I was secretly glad to be safely tied up somewhere and not out in the pass in the dark. 'That's how to do it,' I said to Joss implying the whole thing had been planned.

An early start the next day enabled us to catch the tide through the Active Pass. It was a magnificent day as we sped along with the current. This is one of the classic, tourist brochure, beauty spots on the coast and lived up to its reputation. Beautiful wooded cliffs on either side, seals and gulls feeding in the eddies of the water. Up above, circling in the sky or perched on the trees and cliffs was the largest colony of eagles that I have ever seen.

Joss tried his hand at fishing as we drifted in the sunshine down the shore of Vancouver Island. I inspected his tackle box. The gear was useless, too light, having been designed for fly fishing on the lakes of Saskatchewan. But Joss was enjoying himself.

We headed for the harbour of Oak Bay rather than Victoria. I was not confident I could beat against the wind into the confined spaces of Victoria harbour. Patrick in Vancouver had recommended Oak Bay, to the east, as easy to sail into.

It turned out to be easier said than done. There are two narrow entrances to Oak Bay. I should have chosen the other one. Before I realised it, *Molly B* was in irons – refusing to answer to the tiller and being pushed by the current up on to the rocky breakwater at the entrance to the harbour. With a gentle thud the hull hit the rocks and grounded. The tide was ebbing. There did not seem much danger, as there was no swell to knock *Molly B* against the rocks. The whole thing happened very gently. While it seemed a bit embarrassing to me as the skipper, the solution was simply to row out an anchor and await the turn of the tide.

At the time I did not see the grounding in that calm frame of mind. Thinking I could sail off the mud, I rushed about lowering the sails, raising them again and then lowering them. I launched the dinghy hastily from the deck, damaging it, and then threw the anchor into it, further damaging it. I pushed with the big oar, I tangled ropes, I untangled ropes. I shouted and screamed at Joss, telling him to do ten things at once. I rowed out an anchor but not far enough. It dragged when we pulled against it. The masts slowly leaned over to port. We were stuck fast.

Salvation appeared in the form of a big launch which sped out from the marina, passed us a rope and dragged *Molly B* off. They towed us to a good spot for anchoring and left us to tidy up. Joss was in a cheerful mood while I felt taken down a peg or two. 'I could sure do with a beer,' said Joss as we rowed ashore to check out the sedate, dry, suburb of Oak Bay.

Joss departed the next day. That was the last I saw or heard of him. Not a man for letter writing was Joss. He had to get back to Vancouver to carry on with his career as Canada's 'best known undiscovered artist'. And also to visit his two kids once a week. A better shipmate a man could not ask for, especially when the going got sticky.

I stayed a week in Oak Bay, working on the boat and seeing some of the sights of the city of Victoria. The main mast with its gaff rig needed much attention. Chafe, that traditional problem of gaff-rigged boats, was a large part of the problem. The sails rub against the stays, the stays rub against the gaff, the gaff rubs against the halyards, the halyards rub against the jaws and the jaws rub against the mast. The whole rig tries to self-destruct, needing constant attention. Bits of leather here, a brass pad there, bits of string pulling this way, shims of wood pushing that way. Shock cord, plastic tubing, insulation tape and rags everywhere.

I soaked up the atmosphere of Oak Bay. It has neat gardens and polite schoolchildren. The city of Victoria might have been transplanted from Surrey with its teashops, cream buns and well tended gardens. The museum in the city has a superb display of Pacific Northwest Indian artefacts and totem poles remembering the original inhabitants of the coast.

The boat was deemed ready and on March 12th I set sail. I caught a following wind and tide around the fearsome Race Rocks, the southerly point of Vancouver Island. A beautiful day's sail brought me to Sook inlet and to crown it all I caught a fine salmon along the way by trolling a shiny lure on a 2-kilo weight. 'Now why could I not have done that when Joss was around?' I asked myself.

The following day, appropriately, Friday the 13th, I got an early start in light head winds and beat all day to the west along the north side of the strait of Juan de Fuca. As the day progressed the winds built in strength blowing from ahead. At Point No Point, 9 miles from Sook, I gave up, turned and ran back to Sook for the night. The next day I repeated the exercise but the wind turned a bit more favourable as the day wore on. In a marathon tacking session, reminiscent of the America's Cup, *Molly B* clawed her way through the strait, reaching Neah Bay at the south entrance after nightfall.

I had sailed into Neah Bay before on a delivery trip, so sailing in without a motor was not as difficult in the dark as it might have

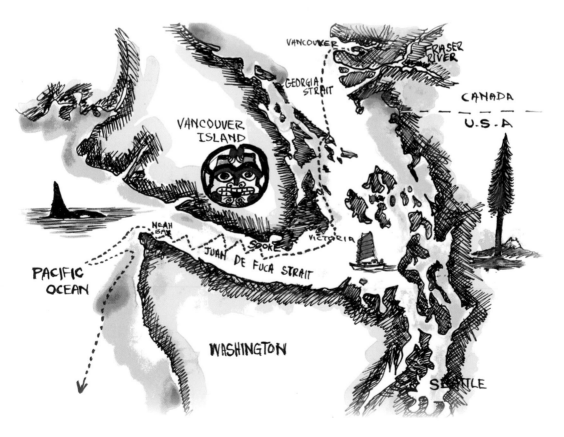

been. It was a Saturday night as I dropped anchor off the small Native American reservation town. It was a bit like a scene from a 1950's cowboy movie ashore as the young bucks roared up and down the main street in jeeps discharging guns into the night sky. I stayed on board.

Neah Bay is well situated, just inside Cape Flattery, the north west tip of continental USA. It is a large, artificially built harbour created by joining off lying Waddah Island to the mainland by a mile long stone causeway. It is an ideal spot for yachts to await fair weather in the Pacific. A US Coast Guard station is based there and nearby is a military early warning station. The land about is native reservation and the local tribe has a tradition of hunting whales, going back to pre-Columbian times.

The Coast Guard came by in a launch and told me not to leave without clearing customs. Other than that I was left to my own devices. *Molly B* stayed a week in the deserted harbour while the winds blew up to gale force. Some rusty fishing boats came in to shelter for a couple of days and I put out a second anchor. I visited the Coast Guard station each day to read their weather report and maps. When I asked the duty officers about sailing south one of them drawled: 'Waall, cap'n, you'd be better off waiting a couple o' months till this thang clears up.'

'He's probably right,' I said to myself. I celebrated St Patrick's Day alone on board with a spaghetti dinner, listened to an Italian opera on the radio while anchored off a Native American reservation with the wind howling in the rigging.

I spent the days storing things, working on the new, largely untested rig and watching the weather. On the eighth day, getting a bit restless, I decided to give it a go.

I checked early at the Coast Guard station and their weather map. There did not appear to be anything too frightening in the way of a disturbance in the area between Japan, Alaska and where I was standing. I decided to sail out and see what it was like.

# 3

# 'Into the Mystic'

*'Hark now hear the sailors cry*
*Smell the sea and feel the sky*
*Let your soul and spirit fly into the mystic.'*

The recommended route for going south in a yacht from the strait of Juan de Fuca is to get well offshore. Harbours to the south are few and usually have bars, which must be crossed, guarding them. In addition, the great Columbia River discharges into the Pacific 120 miles to the south and can cause a disturbance over a wide area. Because of the time of year and without a motor, I intended to stay well offshore.

In grey overcast weather I got underway, sailing out into the Pacific past Cape Flattery and Tatoosh Island. Here I sailed through a pod of grey whales as they cavorted in the shallow water off the island. I took it as a good omen. The wind was in the southeast, no good for going south, but I could sail offshore, which was what I wanted to do.

For three days *Molly B* stood to the west. I was sick as a dog. I suspect it might have been something I ate which caused it, rather than seasickness, or a combination of both. I could only lie on my bunk and change down sails as the wind increased. The boat crashed

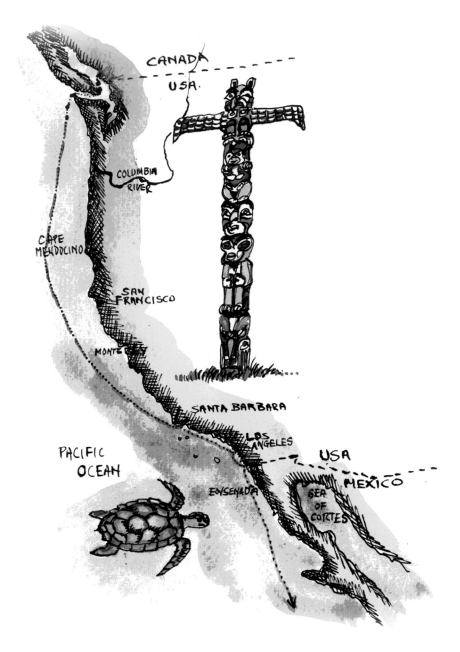

out offshore, west into the Pacific for perhaps 150 miles. I had little idea where we were and cared less. The main sail, furled badly on the boom, damaged itself by rubbing holes through the cloth. I didn't care. The wind increased. I hove to for a day. A passing ship slowed down to check me out. I waved to them and they passed on. In the end, exhausted and despairing of getting a favourable wind, I said 'enough' and turned and headed back towards the east and land. Five days after setting out I found myself back off Cape Flattery again and ready to put back into Neah Bay for a regroup and rest. Suddenly the sun came out and the wind went around to the north. I managed to hold down a bowl of porridge. Things were looking up. I hoisted the torn mainsail and we scudded off to the south.

For the next ten days I sailed down the coasts of Washington, Oregon and California. At times I made good progress, when the wind blew from the north and northwest. At other times I made less than ten miles a day. Sometimes *Molly B* was able to self-steer but more often I had to sit at the tiller and heave to at night. There was one southerly gale where I had to heave to for a day and one northerly blow when I could raise the double reefed main and surge off to the south.

The traffrail log would not work and this was a big loss. It would jam and spin itself into a hopeless mess. The sky was too overcast for celestial navigation most of the time and I was not very practiced at working out sights at this early stage in the voyage. The log would have been a good check on my dead reckoning.

It is worthwhile describing in some detail the chain of events which followed. Sixteen days out from Neah Bay my celestial navigation put *Molly B* off Point Arena, which is 100 miles north of San Francisco. I ran on to the south expecting to pick up Point Reyes with its powerful light marking the northern approaches to San Francisco. I was in sight of the shore and all next day expected to see Point Reyes. A further day's run to the south and I began to realise that I was lost and that I was south of San Francisco bay. Tired and confused I blamed several factors for my predicament: the boat had to heave to each night and drift out to sea, I could not distinguish with certainty any of the shore lights because there were so many of them, and the faulty traffrail log made dead reckoning inaccurate. But lost I was and in sight of shore.

I sailed on and came to a prominent headland by evening but could not positively identify it even when night fell and its powerful flashing light came on. It was more than likely Pigeon Point to the south of San Francisco. I hove to for the night and drifted south. In the morning the headland was out of sight and I was far offshore. I sailed towards the shore. A noon sight put *Molly B* off Monterey Bay. The shore consisted of rocky rugged cliffs. Things were starting to fit into place. I had seen the famous coast of Big Sur often on TV and movies. I ran south along the cliffs all day watching the cars on the road above. By evening I reckoned *Molly B* to be off Cape San Martin and hove to for the night.

The next day, I further confirmed my position by a noon sight and by reading my pilot book, looking at the land and picking out the features. By evening I was identifying the Minutemen rocket silos on the foreshore to the north of Point Arguelo mentioned in my pilot book. Santa Barbara, 40 miles around the point, was the obvious place to head for. 'I will drop anchor in Santa Barbara tomorrow after the toughest sail of my career,' I said to myself. I was tired and confused. It was now the 18th day of the trip. I had expected to be at sea for 10 days.

I hove to for the night. I tacked *Molly B* around at midnight and hove to on the other tack to avoid getting too far offshore. As the dawn broke and the wind died away I could see Point Conception, the dividing line between Northern and Southern California. The sun came up. I could see oil rigs in the distance. It was going to be a scorcher of a day, I thought, as I discarded woolly socks and jumpers. I hauled out my battered sun hat as *Molly B* rounded Point Conception.

There was a strong current sweeping out of the Santa Barbara Channel. I could see this by *Molly B*'s lack of progress along the shore. I headed inshore to avoid the current and to look at the fancy ranch houses that dot the bald green slopes.

By midday the sun was high in the sky, the wind calm and the sails flapping about. I had been on the tiller since before dawn at 4.30 that morning. I ate a huge pancake breakfast and felt dozy. It seemed safe enough to take a nap. I lashed the tiller and dropped the main sail, leaving the genoa and mizzen up. I did not anchor because I thought it might be too deep and did not want to lose one of my nice shiny new anchors. I went below and lay on one of the bunks. I estimated that *Molly B* was about two miles offshore, though from what happened next it might have been less.

Not long after slipping into a deep weary sleep I was roused by the gentle lurch of the boat bumping on something. As I stuck my head out the hatch, it happened again only a little harder. As I looked around I could see that the boat was running straight up on the shore. It was too late to do anything. The hull bumped gently twice again as *Molly B* surged through the surf like a surfboard. Then as she connected firmly with the shore, *Molly B* slewed around broadside on to the waves, keeled over on her side and started to pound on the rocky ledges.

Things looked grim. In fact, it looked like the end of the road for the voyage of the *Molly B*. We had run ashore at a place called Coho, which is just east of Point Conception and, ironically, a recommended anchorage. There was virtually no wind but quite a swell running, a thing quite common on the coast of California. The *Molly B* was grounded on flat rocky ledges that extended from the beach below some low cliffs. There did not appear to be any houses nearby.

It is easy now to describe the scene calmly but at the time things were confused and happening at breakneck speed. *Molly B* became firmly lodged on the flat sandstone rocks, beam on to the incoming waves. There were deep fissures in between the rocks, through which the water rushed and gurgled. Each incoming wave would take the hull of the boat and, pivoting it on the keel, crash it down on the inshore side, the rocks pounding a hole in the starboard side. The outgoing wave would have the reverse effect, pivoting the hull back on to its other side, the masts and the rigging describing a broad arc through the air. Then the next incoming wave would begin the process again. There was confusion everywhere, ropes and sails and bits of equipment tossed all over the decks and cabin. I had to hold tight to a mast or rail to stop myself being thrown off the deck.

At first the hull bounced clear when on top of the waves and I thought that if I could get an anchor out into deep water I might have a chance of hauling the boat off. I launched the 9 foot dinghy from its position on top of the cabin. The next incoming wave filled it and capsized it. I jumped into the water. I could stand on the giant flat rocks, the water up to my waist. I had to be careful not to get caught

under the hull as it came flying across with the waves. I brought the dinghy ashore through the surf thinking to bail it out and try again. But I could see that it was useless. *Molly B* was stuck fast, a majestic and frightening sight as only such disasters as shipwrecks can be. The swell whooshed in relentlessly and the hull pivoted on its keel each time and pounded down on the rocks. The masts, swinging like a giant inverted pendulum were still standing. I was amazed that the rigging was taking the strain.

A girl with two kids came up the beach. In true Californian style she empathised with me, telling me that she knew how bad it must feel to crash my boat! She said the nearest phone was in a house some miles away. She said she would go and call the Coast Guard.

I went back on board. I was convinced now that the boat was doomed. The water was starting to slosh about above the floorboards. The hull would fill with water before anything could be done to save it while it still floated. Then it would be smashed to smithereens in the surf and on the rocks. I gathered a sail bag full of valuables. The radio, my camera, the sextant and the log. A sleeping bag for if I had to camp on the beach.

Just then I noticed a small boat offshore, bobbing about beyond the line of surf. There were two people on board and they were shouting and waving at me. I waved at them and shouted back. 'Call the Coast Guard,' I yelled. 'Call the Coast Guard.' I assumed they had a radio.

We continued shouting at each other but the distance was such that proper communication was impossible. They seemed to be telling me to get on my radio but did not realise that *Molly B* did not have one.

I got out the longest rope on board – over 200 feet long. I attached it to the bow of *Molly B* and swam out through the surf towards the small blue boat. I was still quite far from it when I came to the end of the rope. I shouted for them to come in a bit closer. It seemed to me to be deep enough. The men in the boat attached a line to a large

buoy and floated it off in the water. There was not wind or waves enough to make the buoyed rope move in my direction. It was off to the side. I was getting tired and cold as I treaded water at the end of my rope. I started to fear that I might drown. I abandoned the rope and swam back to *Molly B.* Just hoisting my exhausted body back on board was difficult. My knees could hardly support my body; they had turned to rubber.

*Molly B* was still pounding heavily on the starboard side and seemed to have been moved up the beach into shallower water. The hull would only now pivot when a particularly large roller came sweeping in. Below in the cabin the mess was indescribable, water sloshing everywhere freely.

I began to think that the Coast Guard was the only hope of being pulled off the beach. I looked out at the small blue boat beyond the surf and thought that even if I did get a line to them the boat could not be powerful enough to pull *Molly B* off. 'Probably a couple of amateur fishermen out for an afternoon's fishing,' I thought. 'They won't understand the problems of what's involved here.' Their boat looked very small, only a speedboat. I shouted vainly out to them to get help.

There was nothing much I could do except hang on to the pounding *Molly B*. I started to tidy up the mess of ropes and sails. I dropped the genoa and mizzen sails, which were still up. The surf continued to roll in. I was resigned to the loss of the boat and my dream. It was all over unless the Coast Guard arrived.

Then, like an angel sent by the Lord, in through the surf swam one of the men. 'Hello. Hello, matie,' he said with the accent of a London bobby. 'What's going on here?' He hauled himself on board. Called Ray and wearing a wet suit he explained that the blue boat called *Moki* could not come any closer as it had a deep propeller which might get damaged in the shallows. Ray had swum in with a line as far as it would go and left a buoy on the end of it between *Moki* and *Molly B*. Together we joined two anchor lines and Ray swam back out with them and connected with the line to Moki.

*Moki* turned and faced out to sea, the line attached to her stern. Slowly the strain came on the rope. *Molly B* was still bouncing clear

of the bottom on the crest of large waves. *Moki* revved up, her stern digging into the sea, exhaust smoke swirling up and her bow lifting as the strain came on the rope. Slowly the bow of *Molly B* turned and faced out to sea. As each roller swept in and lifted the hull clear of the rocks she started to move, slowly at first. With much yelling and whooping from the crew of *Moki*, like cowboys at a rodeo, off bounced *Molly B* and slid out through the surf into deep water.

It was getting late in the afternoon and dusk was starting to fall. The two boats tied alongside and cleared their lines. Jon the captain and owner of *Moki* introduced himself. He was an abalone diver and Ray was his helper. They were very excited to have pulled the hull off the rocks, as was I to be rescued. Jon was kept busy talking on his radio to the Coast Guard who were following proceedings blow by blow. 'There's a coast guard cutter and a helicopter on its way,' said Jon. I could not have been in better hands.

In the cabin of *Molly B* the water was well above the floorboards and the hull was visibly settling in the sea below the waterline. I started pumping with the bilge pump. Ray came aboard and helped. We took it in turns. The 30 gallon a minute bilge pump plus a bucket could just keep up with the flow. 'The chopper will bring a pump,' said Jon. We tried stretching a sail over the hull around the keel to slow the intake but it did not have much effect. I had read about that trick in my Hornblower books.

Jon was in contact with the Coast Guard, which was on its way. As the chopper approached, the two boats separated. They would drop the pump on to *Moki* as there were no masts or rigging to obstruct things. Just as darkness was falling the chopper arrived. It was a powerful sight as it hovered over the little blue boat 50 meters away from *Molly B*. It reminded me of movies about the Vietnam War. There were lights blazing, strobes flashing, rotors roaring, turbines whining and a circle of waves whipped up on the surface of the water. The crew of the chopper, in white helmets and dark shades, peered down inscrutably, like spacemen.

Two pumps, packed in large steel drums, were lowered on to the deck of *Moki* and the chopper sped off into the night back to Los Angeles. *Moki* moved back alongside *Molly B* and all three of us lifted one of the pumps on board. 'They give you two in case one does not work,' explained Jon.

It took us some time to get the petrol-driven pump working. We had to prime it using a kettle. Then, once working, it cleared the bilge in a matter of minutes. By now it was dark.

'Let's go,' said Jon.

We rigged a towline from *Molly B* to *Moki*. I found a replacement for the tiller on *Molly B*. The tiller had snapped when the boat hit the beach. We set off for Santa Barbara, which was 30 miles away and *Moki's* home port.

Ray stayed on board *Molly B* as it needed one man to steer and another to operate the pump every 15 minutes or so. It took five hours to reach Santa Barbara, *Molly B* surging along at her hull speed of about six knots. *Moki*, a light displacement 25 foot planing speedboat with a powerful inboard/outboard motor, could normally expect to make about 25 knots, so progress was slow by her standards.

We reached Santa Barbara at 2 o'clock in the morning and tied up *Molly B* in the travel lift of the boat yard. 'See you in the morning,' said Jon as he took off in his truck. I catnapped for the rest of the night, operating the Coast Guard pump every half hour or so to keep *Molly B* afloat. Tired and in a dazed, zombie-like state, I realised that the boat had been saved. What luck! Snatched from the jaws of Davy Jones's Locker. The voyage wasn't over yet.

# 4

# 'No Cash, No Splash'

*'No cash, No splash.*
*No mon, No fun*
*No beans, No scenes'*

Dawn broke on the artificial flood lights of the marina. Early risers shuffled to work. The smell of fresh coffee and doughnuts mingled with the smell of diesel fumes, dead fish and the sea. The sun rises in a haze over the southern Californian mountains. Another early day in Santa Barbara Marina dawned.

When the boat yard opened the travel lift arrived. Positioning slings under *Molly B*, the yard workers efficiently lifted the spouting hull clear of the water. They carried it dripping to the nearby Rod's boat yard. There it was propped up in a cradle. I could at last relax. I wandered around the harbour waterfront, found a diner and had a huge American breakfast.

The scarred boat attracted a lot of attention and I had to explain my story to a steady stream of onlookers from the boats around and visitors to the yard. As things quietened down about midday I crawled into my bunk for a nap.

It took the next two days to sort and dry things and take stock of the situation. The damage to *Molly B* was serious. The hull was holed badly below the waterline just aft of amidships on the starboard side. Here the boat had taken the brunt of the pounding and a section of the hull about the size of a car wheel had been totally worn away. The pliable layer of insulation, fibreglassed to the interior of the hull, had saved the boat from sinking. It had caved in rather than breaking. Inside the cabin some bulkheads had been stove in with the pounding. Other, lesser damage had occurred to the sole of the keel and here and there on the hull, mainly on the starboard side. The rudder had taken quite a hammering and a big section of it had been worn away.

I saw a lot of Jon and Ray and their friends the abalone divers. Jon was justly proud of his efforts in hauling me off the beach, saving *Molly B* and possibly my life. He was entitled to claim salvage against *Molly B*. As a commercial fisherman making his living from the sea no one would have thought it unfair of him to do so. Instead, he treated me like a brother, refused any offer of reward for what he had done and insisted on helping me repair the boat.

'You're going to sail to Ireland?' he asked. 'Far out man! We'll soon have you back in the water.' He had built his own boat, *Moki*. Now he arrived down to the boat yard with his power tools and started helping repair *Molly B*.

I felt more like quitting the venture myself. 'What was the point?' I thought. I had made a right mess of things. My nice new boat was in bits, I was lucky not to have lost it completely, and it would cost a fortune to repair. Then to launch it and head off without a motor seemed to be asking for the same thing all over again. Why not walk away from it now?

But the repair took on its own momentum. The fact that Jon was helping me rather than hassling me made a big difference. We marked out the area of the hull which had to be ground back, an oval patch six feet long and four feet high. An actual hole about two feet in diameter had to be cut away completely. I spent a good five days doing preparation work – grinding, sanding and chiselling at the hull in the Californian sun. Before the new fibreglass repair could be applied the hull would have to be tilted over on its side. Ideally it should be turned up side down, but we decided we could manage by simply tilting the hull over to port. Before this could be done the masts had to be removed. To do this Jon rounded up all his buddies in the abalone diving business and they manhandled the masts out of *Molly B* as she stood – this to avoid hiring a crane. Then the travel lift picked up *Molly B* and, in a series of gentle manoeuvres, laid the hull over on its side. I had been living in the hull as I worked on it – an uncomfortable and itchy experience. The fibreglass dust gets everywhere. Now I continued living in the hull as it rested on its side at an angle of 50 degrees.

Fibreglass is a forgiving substance, easy to repair. With the hull tilted over it was a reasonably easy task to cut the fibreglass cloth to its proper shape, wet it out with resin and apply it to the hull like a huge medical dressing. Each layer overlapped the one before and the final layer was a skin of closely woven cloth to make the finish as smooth as possible. Then the process was repeated inside the hull building the thickness up to greater than the original. Jon was convinced that the repaired hull was stronger than the original. Then I got to work sanding and fairing the patched hull until it was not possible to tell that the hull had been holed at all.

Other, smaller damaged areas of the hull and the rudder I attended to at the same time, filling, glassing and fairing. The hot sun of the Californian spring made it possible to apply several applications of fibreglass each day.

The hull was now ready to be set standing back upright by the travel lift. I could now start to rebuild the interior where I had removed everything on the starboard side. The heavy, bolted together style of construction which I used when fitting out the hull made this task reasonably easy.

I saw less of Jon as he went back to his work diving for abalone and urchins. He introduced me to all his friends and I became a bit of a character around the waterfront of Santa Barbara, a waterfront renowned for its characters, be they ageing film stars or retired millionaires. At the bottom of the stratum in Santa Barbara are the people who have to work for a living such as Jon.

There were tensions between the fishermen of Santa Barbara and the conservationists, particularly over protecting the endangered sea otter whose favourite food is abalone. It also happened to be one of the favourite foods of film stars and the wealthy residents of Santa Barbara. The wealthy residents also happened to be conservationists because it was fashionable. Fishermen felt that they were the victims of a dastardly plot to eliminate them and that the sea otter was more important than their traditional livelihood. In the centre of this argument fell the shipwrecked *Molly B*, which was being assisted by a fisherman, a noble deed by one who would have liked to see the sea otter population controlled. By helping *Molly B*, Jon was saying that he was compassionate towards humans while not really caring for the plight of the sea otter. *Molly B* inadvertently became a cause on the side of the fishermen.

The only thing Jon had really wanted to do in his life was be in the air force and fly planes in Viet Nam. For some reason he failed to do that. Then he had been into motorbikes. This explained the slight limp he had. He had once tried to outrun a police car but the cops 'had cheated'. 'They radioed ahead and they were waiting for me,' he explained. They had rammed him on his bike with a patrol car. Then he had taken up diving. He pulled up his shirt to reveal a large scar in a V shape across his stomach and chest. 'Shark caught me in the Farallon Islands. Coast Guard saved my life just like they saved yours.' Then he had built the 25 foot *Moki* and taken up abalone diving.

In all, *Molly B* was out of the water in the boatyard for about five weeks. It was not all work during that time. Jon's girlfriend Susie and her family adopted me and invited me on many outings. Their idea of fun was to go up to the canyons above Santa Barbara and fire off shots from a collection of civil war arms while dressed in period costume.

Another good friend of Jon's called Captain Jack was a sea captain who did contract work on oil rig supply vessels all over the world. That is, when not hanging around on the waterfront at Santa Barbara. He was not very impressed with the voyage of the *Molly B*, especially my plans to sail down to Central America. 'You don't know what it's like down there. I do,' he drawled. 'They'll kill you, they'll take your boat. You ain't got a chance. Get yourself a gun. Get a radio. Get a motor in this vessel,' he ordered. He was sort of old school – an ugly American condemned to live in the hotels of Santa Barbara in order to avoid various wives. We became good friends. One day he frog-marched me down to the marine store in Santa Barbara and bought me all the charts and publications I needed to sail to Panama.

Launch day approached. I scraped together all the money I had, even selling some books out of the ship's library. But it was not enough. Rod's boatyard had a motto which was writ large on a sign at the entrance: 'NO CASH – NO SPLASH.' I had to swallow my pride and call my dad in Ireland and get him to bail me out. An anxious few days of running around to post offices, telephones and banks and Rod had his cash. *Molly B* was ready for her splash.

The travel lift arrived. It was a wonderful launching. Jon gave up his day's fishing to be there. Other friends gathered and a lively party developed. Guest of honour was a Newfoundland bagpiper. The clan gathered behind the piper who gathered behind the travel lift and we marched in procession across the yard as the pipes drowned out the roar of the lift. Jon insisted on smashing a bottle of his beloved Coors

beer over the bows, the pipes struck up 'Over the sea to Skye' and
*Molly B* was gently lowered back down into the water.

The party continued as we stepped the masts. I was glad enough
as people faded away. I could get on with tightening up the rigging
and all the endless refitting, stowing and tidying up involved in a
launch. The harbour police moved *Molly B* to a marina berth for a
few days where I completed the commissioning. Then early one
morning, when no one was looking and it was calm, I towed *Molly
B* with the dinghy outside the harbour to the anchorage and there I
stayed for another week.

I painted a picture of Jon's boat *Moki* that had rescued *Molly B*. I framed the picture and gave it to him. It was the least that I could do for him after all he had done for me. To Ray I gave some money. Jon was pleased. He was a bit mixed up about the Irish shamrock. He thought it the same thing as the lucky four leaf clover. It was too complicated to explain to him that the four leaf clover has little to do with St Patrick's shamrock which was used to convert the pagan Irish to Christianity. But he insisted that *Molly B* should have a four leaf shamrock painted on her stern for good luck. And that is why *Molly B* had a four leaf Shamrock painted on her stern.

Three of my Santa Barbara friends, Jake, Allan and John, signed up for a sail down the coast to Los Angeles. We set sail loaded down to the gunnels with Kentucky Fried Chicken. Ray, who had swum in through the surf to rescue *Molly B*, came down to say good bye. 'You'll be all right now,' he said. 'You've had your smash up and survived.'

It was a slow trip down the coast to Long Beach. The wind dropped at dusk and rather than mess about in the Santa Barbara Channel at night in misty conditions we crept inshore and dropped anchor off the entrance to Port Hueneme. There, the howling of seals kept us awake all night. Another full day of windless sailing and my guests were getting impatient, suggesting that I put them ashore on a beach and they would catch a bus back to Santa Barbara. We took nine hours to cover the final eight miles to Long Beach. I dropped anchor next door to the Queen Mary liner and my guests rushed ashore in the morning muttering, 'How can he do it.'

I was equally relieved to be on my own again. Alone and in one piece, so to speak. Santa Barbara had been kind to me and I do not want to sound ungrateful. I had to get away from it because people were too kind.

I spent over two weeks in the Los Angeles harbour area and wish I had stayed a little longer in this exciting city. At times I did a bit of sightseeing in the city and at others worked on the boat. I found an old style marine instrument shop in San Pedro, the old traditional port of Los Angeles, and tried to get the Walker log fixed. Whatever they did to it, they did not fix it. My nice Sony short wave radio was a casualty of the shipwreck. I was able to find a cheap short wave radio which I used for the rest of the voyage to get time signals, essential for celestial navigation.

I was still doubtful about continuing the trip. In fact, I tried to sell the boat in Los Angeles. Perhaps it was all the marinas and boat brokers I noticed about the city. I found a broker who seemed interested when I told him I had a Tahiti ketch for sale. He dealt in traditional boats. He came over to Long Beach to see *Molly B*. He examined the cabin and his face dropped. 'Where's the bathroom, where's the motor? I can't sell a boat without a bathroom.' He was shocked when I told him that I stood on the fore deck and threw a bucket of shit overboard. He could not get ashore quick enough.

Anchored at Long Beach in the shadow of the great liner *Queen Mary* was one of the more interesting places *Molly B* has visited. The *Queen* is converted into a hotel and I was able to wander on board

and inspect the art deco interior. In true Hollywood fashion, out-of-work actors would perform the changing of the guard outside the entrance each hour in a caricature of the real London thing, which no longer takes place, outside Buckingham Palace.

I left Los Angeles on June 16th, Bloomsday. It was not such a lucky day for me as it had been for Joyce. When I tried to raise the anchor it was fouled in the soupy waters of Long Beach harbour. Being calm I could not use the natural rocking of the boat to break out the anchor. Using an elaborate system of pulleys, hooks, sheet winches and two hours of running back and forth I managed to haul it slowly to the surface. It appeared to be hooked around the telephone cable for the entire city of LA. I tied a rope around the cable, untangled the anchor and consigned the rest to the murk. I hoped I did not disconnect anyone as I set sail, at flat calm speed, for San Diego.

The distance to San Diego is about 80 miles and it was to take four tiring days of lolling about in flat calm conditions to get there. The first day brought *Molly B* to an anchor off the beach at San Clemente, 25 miles down the coast. There was no sign of the most famous local resident, ex-President Richard Nixon, walking on the beach.

I awoke the next morning to find the boat a bit close to a low tide reef. I set sail in light and variable winds. An informal race developed with a sloop which came up from behind and passed *Molly B*. I experimented with a mizzen staysail for the first time and it seemed to improve speed. That night I tied up to a big buoy off a place called Carlsbad where there is a power station. The local seals kept me awake all night and poor *Molly B* kept drifting on to the giant steel buoy and banging on it. An uncomfortable night.

I got a very early start the third day of this 80 mile marathon. The wind filled in from the southeast blowing quite fresh. A dead header. There was nothing for it but to beat into it. Twelve hours later and 18 hard won miles along the shore I dropped anchor off the fishing pier at the entrance to a place called Mission Bay. There I spent another uncomfortable rolly night. The next morning, day four, I completed

the five miles to the entrance to San Diego harbour. *Molly B* rounded
Point Loma and sailed in among the exercising war ships. San Diego,
as well as being the HQ for sailing on the west coast, is also the head-
quarters of the Pacific fleet of the US Navy. I found a little gaggle of
cruising boats, dropped anchor among them and had a rest.

*Molly B* stayed in San Diego harbour for over three months. I had
discovered that further to the south it was the hurricane season. Local boats avoid the coast of Mexico during the summer months and I
was not in the mood for any further heroics. I had had a close call in
Santa Barbara; there was no point in pushing my luck further. There
was nothing for it but to wait out the three months until September
and then head south.

San Diego is an interesting place to hang around if one is into
boats, as I was. The time flew. There was much to be done to *Molly
B*. There always was. I saw the sights of the town of San Diego and
quickly exhausted them. At times I regretted not staying longer in
Los Angeles but San Diego is more convenient for living on board a
boat. There is a huge floating live-aboard population in the harbour. I
even met some friends from Vancouver. At Coronado across the bay
there was a floating village of multihulls, most of which looked as if
they had been designed by NASA. One rarely saw any of them go out
sailing; they seemed to concentrate on growing plants on their extensive decks. At Shelter Island, the real cruisers congregated, again in a
floating village. Here there were boatyards and marine stores, yacht
clubs, big name yacht designers, brokers and sail makers.

Three miles up the harbour was an anchorage off downtown San
Diego. It was mainly filled with derelicts and no-hope, abandoned,
dream ships. I anchored for a while beside someone living in a floating box! Such is the overcrowding and demand for space in the harbour of San Diego that there is a municipal rule about anchoring.
There are certain designated anchorages where a boat can anchor for
free but such boats must display a light at night. This is a good rule
for it insures that boats are attended and not neglected. Boats not

displaying the required light can be towed away just like an illegally parked car.

I divided my time between Shelter Island and the anchorage off downtown San Diego. Tony, an old enemy from Vancouver, on his steel tri, *The Ways of Magic*, ruled the roost in Shelter Island, living in the centre of the floating raft-up in the inner basin. He was doing great business making and selling wind generators for boats. It was the early days of wind generators and Tony had twigged to the fact that you could take an ordinary motor car generator, attach a wind propeller to it, haul it up the forestay of a yacht and it would charge a battery. Tony would make the 1.5 metre props out of wood and supply all the other parts in a kit. Things were going fine and he was talking about expanding into a factory when I first met him. Then one day one of his customers walked into one of his whizzing, invisible, propellers as it was generating up on a foredeck and badly damaged his face. The last time I saw Tony he was talking to insurance companies. Wind generators now have much more compact propellers and professional installations.

I went into business also, painting boat portraits and marine paintings around San Diego.

I had moments of depression in San Diego as I awaited the passing of the hurricane season. I even tried to sell *Molly B* again. There was not much response to an ad in a local yachting paper. In retrospect it seems like a daft idea, to have survived the crash in Santa

Barbara, repaired the boat and then try to sell it. As September approached and with the end of the hurricane season, the idea faded.

I prepared for sea. Another of the rules of the harbour in San Diego is that you cannot dry out a boat on any of the beaches in the harbour. This I might have considered doing as the underwater bottom of *Molly B* was already showing signs of growth in the warm, nutrient-laden waters of the harbour. Hauling out in any of the boatyards seemed out of the question for financial reasons. I dived in and cleaned the hull with a scraper, but no doubt removed a lot of the anti-fouling paint in the process.

I stocked up the larder as best I could. A neighbouring single-hander convinced me that I should salt my own pork. It was my own fault for having read so much about the British Navy and hard tack and early single handed sailors that I attempted it. I bought a catering pack of bacon and a load of salt in a supermarket. I mixed up the two and stored it in a plastic container in the bilge. It was to prove a terrible waste of money and energy. Other provisioning was of a more ordinary nature – cans and packets, jars and bottles slowly sourced and ferried on board. I took on water, looked over my charts, cleared the decks and was ready to go.

The long haul down to Panama was ready to begin.

# 5

# 'Day after Day, Day after Day'

*'Day after day, day after day,*
*We stuck, nor breath nor motion;*
*As idle as a painted ship*
*Upon a painted ocean.'*

The hurricane season off the coast of Mexico to the south was ending. The voyage could begin again. Hopefully the false start and the nightmare of the beach at Santa Barbara were behind. Mexico, the coast of Central America and Panama were ahead. There was still a slight chance of an end-of-season hurricane but I was keen to get going in the engineless *Molly B*. The plan once again was to head offshore and make as much southing as possible.

Winds were light as *Molly B* drifted out through the fleet of warships and submarines which litter San Diego harbour. Two days of drifting in the sun brought me to the smelly, pelican-infested harbour of Ensenada, a busy fish processing centre.

I had hoped to 'clear' into Mexico at Ensenada and thus present my bona fides to the dreaded Mexican officialdom. Tales from the US side of the border about the horrors of the Mexican people, army, navy and red tape were rife. I had been advised by everyone to carry a gun and use it. In a fit of worry I had even bought a sport

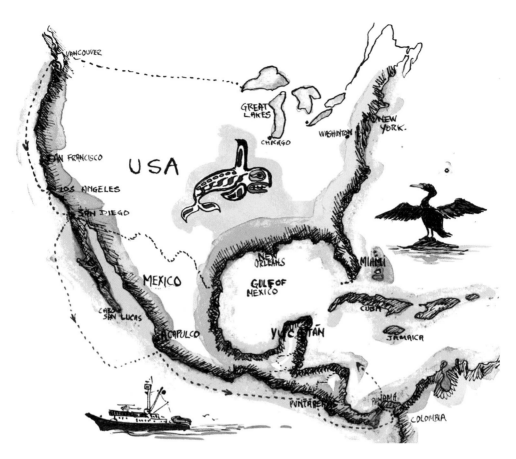

fishing licence for Mexican waters – a scam run by the fishing tackle shops of San Diego in cahoots with the Mexican consul. Now, here in Ensenada, the officials did not appear to be interested in *Molly B*, or the Q flag I flew.

The tuna clippers came and went all day and night, unloading in a blaze of searchlights and the roar of generators. The huge frozen fish were hauled out of the holds of the tuna clippers by the tail with cranes, ice steam swirling up into the air. Everywhere was the smell of rotting fish. The pelicans munched away on the guts and offal from the processing plants. Then they messed up all over the boats in the harbour on which they perched. I had difficulty getting rid of a family of them which took up residence in the dinghy tied to the

stern. Ensenada was a mess. A town rapidly becoming a guano deposit.

I was even more concerned with the mosquitos. They were everywhere. They found the cabin of *Molly B*, liked it, invited their friends and moved in. They thought I tasted delicious. The first night I did not sleep at all. In the morning I rushed ashore and bought the wherewithal to make some screens then spent the day industriously knocking them together. Essential equipment.

Four days in Ensenada with the mosquitos, smells, pelicans and bumboats was enough for me. I got the all clear on the hurricane front from the radio and I was gone. Destination – as far south as the winds would carry *Molly B*.

The nicest way to sail south would have been to visit the many bays and anchorages on the Baja peninsula, California's playground in Mexico. On the tip of the peninsula is the famous Cabo San Lucas, an important yachting Mecca. But I decided to go offshore, avoiding the shipping, the shoreline and the worry of a late hurricane. I would head for the port of Puntarenas in Costa Rica, another popular cruising stopover. The west coast of Mexico is longer than the west coast of the USA, some 2,000 miles as opposed to about 1,400 miles for continental USA. After that there were the coasts of inhospitable Guatemala, El Salvador and Nicaragua, where civil war was raging. More than 2,000 miles of calms, variable winds, tropical storms and burning sun lay ahead. A further 1,000 miles with the added danger of shipping would bring *Molly B* to Panama.

*Molly B* tacked all day in light winds across the bay of Todos Santos on which Ensenada is situated. As if to confirm my offshore strategy I had a narrow escape creeping past the rocks at the exit to the bay – Cabo Punta Banda. The sails flopped about uselessly on their heavy spars. I frantically rowed with the steering oar pushing just clear of the surf. 'Get offshore and away from all this,' I said to myself.

A further day of drifting and the land was still in sight. The following day it was out into the calm glassy stretches of the Pacific Ocean.

For the first couple of nights I tried sleeping on deck in the warm tropical nights. This might enable me to hear the approach of a ship and take avoiding action if a collision seemed imminent. We were in the busy shipping lanes running down the west coast from the industrial north to the Panama canal. There was also much fishing boat traffic. The tuna clippers, with their rakish bows and helicopter spotters, buzzed here and there. I put a cushion on the side deck and bunked down under a space blanket. The side decks of *Molly B* with the high gunnels to one side and the boxy cabin to the other are just the right size. Like sleeping out under the stars when camping, it takes a bit of getting used to.

The voyage turned into a slow motion nightmare. *Molly B* made dismal progress in the light winds. At times we made less than 15 miles a day. Winds were light, variable or non-existent. There were sudden rain showers and sail-ripping squalls. The sun blasted down mercilessly. In contrast, wind came as two disturbances, hurricane Norma and tropical storm Otis, passed to the south. Anxiously, I listened to the short wave radio and plotted the storm positions on the chart. There was no need to worry though. The disturbance was far to the south and provided some well needed winds for a couple of days.

All the fresh food rotted in the tropical conditions. I lived on pancakes and Aunt Jemima's maple syrup, bully beef and spaghetti. Like a flock of vultures, a family of boobies, the dark, gannet-like birds of the tropics, took up residence on the mast tops and proceeded to make a terrible mess of the deck. What an insult! They would not do that to a racing boat. In the gentle motion they just sat there out of range of everything I could throw at them. I shook the halyards, shouted, banged and threw missiles of firewood, all to no avail. *Molly B* took on some of the aspects of the raft of the Medusa (or is it the Hesperus) as she lumbered along, weeds trailing astern from the hull, boobies perched in the rigging and crew wiped out from sun, indolence and boredom.

Twenty-two days out from Ensenada there was still 1,500 miles to go to Punta Arenas in Costa Rica. I was worried about pushing things too hard again and getting into trouble. My main concern was about the food running out completely. The nearest good port was Acapulco, 600 miles inshore. So I headed for there. It seemed the best thing to do. Have a rest, restock the ship's larder and try again.

*Molly B* was averaging 60 miles a day. Progress was even slower as I back tracked to Acapulco, taking 14 days to reach the Mexican coast.

The statistics for the stage speak for themselves. From Ensenada to Acapulco should be 1,350 miles as the seagull flies. I had managed to sail a distance of 2,139 miles in 32 days, an average of 66 miles a day to cover that distance. It's a bit of a round about way to get to Acapulco. Subsequent stages on the way to Panama were to prove even more frustrating.

The city of Acapulco nestles in the corner of what must be one of the safest and most beautiful harbours in the world. One can still imagine it as a Spanish fortress from the days of the conquistadors, the batteries on the headlands anxiously scanning the horizon for signs of the English buccaneers. It lost its importance as a port fol-

lowing the building of the railroad across the Isthmus of Panama when gold was discovered in California in 1849.

Fast forward to the 1950s and film stars and their entourage discovered it and it became the Havana of the West Coast. Fancy hotels, cabaret acts, the beach and game fishing were the attractions. The boom years of the fifties had passed and these hotels had now located south of the town. The city centre had become a colourful slum of run-down apartment buildings and decaying hotels. The waterfront was teeming with street life. Small boys would dive for coins. They offered to mind my dinghy when I went ashore then used it as a diving platform. I had to pay them to retrieve the oarlocks from the bottom of the harbour.

There were no other cruising yachts in Acapulco while *Molly B* was there. This seemed a bit strange to me. A local entrepreneur on the beach near where *Molly B* was anchored had a speed boat. He rented out water ski jaunts to the local Mexican holiday makers and used *Molly B* as a turning mark on the course. Perhaps he was renting out trips to see the amusing yacht. All to the accompaniment of blaring rock music. After two days of attempting to work on the mast while this water ski circus proceeded I was feeling less enthusiastic about the charms of historic old Spanish ports.

I gorged on fresh food, my body soaking up the meat, bread, salads and fruit. I would visit the local butcher shop and rush back to the boat with a huge chunk of fresh steak, wash it down with a carton of fresh milk or orange juice, burp, then crash out in the cabin for the afternoon.

I experimented with the local sausages and cheeses, trying to find one which would last in the tropical heat. Most fresh produce, stored under refrigerated conditions in the shops, will not last very well when brought on board a boat. Potatoes, onions and oranges are your only man. Based on progress so far, I knew I was facing perhaps another month at sea in the blistering heat. I was concerned about what the strange diet might do to me physically. I had dreams of emaciated bodies being taken from life rafts following shipwreck. All my teeth might fall out. This was not supposed to be how people went yachting.

In all, *Molly B* spent a week in Acapulco. I met very few and befriended no one. I did much work on the boat. The rig needed constant attention. The sails were just starting to wear themselves in. As I was to do many other times, I made adjustments to the gaff of the main sail. The gaff jaws, where the gaff meets the mast and forks around it to either side, is a finicky bit of equipment, the Achilles heel of the gaff rig. I outsmarted the water skiers by climbing the mast and working on it early in the morning.

Other important work on the boat was to scrape the underwater hull. The antifouling paint applied in Santa Barbara six months ago now seemed pretty well ineffective in the warm water of the tropics. All the nasty little organisms *Molly B* had picked up in the nutrient-laden waters of San Diego harbour were now thriving, multiplying, cross-fertilising and mutating no doubt in the warm tropical waters. I dived with my mask and snorkel and attacked them with a scraper. I am sure they only laughed at me.

Somewhat rested, adjusted, scraped and stocked up with Mexican sausage meat, *Molly B* set sail from Acapulco in company with the Ecuadorian Sail training vessel, *Guayas*, a fully rigged ship. *Guayas* exited in fine style, rigging and spars decked out with uniformed

trainees, guns saluting. *Molly B* left with less formality, indeed secrecy, for I still had not bothered the hard-working Mexican customs authorities with my presence in their waters.

*Molly B* sailed out into one of the hottest, calmest, most serene stretches of ocean in the world. No wonder it is called the Pacific Ocean. It is in the lee of the high land mass of Central America. There is less wind there than in the doldrums. It is an ocean rich in life and colour. Dolphin and tuna gambol in the sun. The giant manta ray leaps out of the water and belly flops with a mighty explosion. The whales come here to mate. The rain squalls come and go in vast arc-shaped cloud formations. The sun presides over all. At night the stars twinkle, the moon comes and goes. There are few seabirds. Those there are stay near shore and grow fat on the plentiful supply of food. They are big birds – cormorants, pelicans, boobies and frigate birds.

Progress was dismal. Within a week most of the fresh food from Acapulco had rotted and I was back to concocting pea stews, the immortal pancakes and fish when I could catch it.

I would steer all day in the hot sun adjusting the sails depending on the wind direction, sitting in the cockpit, usually reading a book. The current was a big factor. In the marginal conditions a favourable current in the right direction would mean that the apparent wind would be high enough to fill the sails and *Molly B* would make progress. On the other hand, a contrary current slowing down the already slow progress of the boat could stop progress altogether as the sails flop about in the swells. The heavy gaff would flail about slamming the rigging and chaffing the ropes, sails and wits. I became expert at raising and lowering the mainsail and genoa, and knowing when progress was possible and when I simply had to drop sails, go below and rest.

It was difficult to maintain concentration, to keep struggling against the calms, the sun, the heat and the vast area of ocean to be covered. To struggle all morning with sails and sheets, shock cord and tiller just to gain, perhaps, three miles seemed meaningless against the hundreds left to cover. Like the weed-clogged hull I became indolent and sluggish. It was easier to rest in the cabin, read books and cook than to struggle against the fickle elements. I stopped caring. Cargo ships slipped past on the glassy sea. At times they were so close I could read their names and home ports. I did not care if they ran *Molly B* down . . .

At other times I would pull myself together, trim the sails, make minor adjustments and creep along in the light airs like a racing boat in the Solent. I would jump overboard and clean the hull with a scraper, nervously looking about for sharks. A breeze would fill in on the vast, slimy, mirror-top sea. I would boom out the genoa, tie preventers on all the spars, row the stern around to face the right direction with the sculling oar and off we would go. Sometimes we would gain a mile, sometimes less.

At night I would go to bed and sleep. The night seemed too endless to keep up the struggle. I dropped the sails, lashed the tiller and went to my bunk.

In such a fashion I made the busy port of Puntarenas in Costa Rica. There was a welcome pile of letters for me in the post office. My dad, worried about my welfare on the high seas, had sent me some money.

Puntarenas was a happy, busy, chaotic sort of place, popular with yachts as a stopover or a place to do maintenance. The people, though poor, had smiles on their faces. Inflation in Costa Rica was rampant. Anyone who had dollars was in a good position. The yachties spoke of little else except the bargains to be had for those with money.

There was a daily open market in the town centre near the water and I could row over in my dinghy and stock up on pineapples, bananas and super local coffee. The natives did much the same thing in their dugout canoes, using the river as a highway into the overgrown interior. The yachties worked on their boats using the cheap local labour and hardwoods. One boat being restored was the 150 foot three-masted schooner Bertha of Ibiza! At night the anchorage was blasted by the sound of the local bands with their accordions, guitars and drums.

I left after ten days for the final leg to the Panama Canal. Once again, progress was slow. This time I stayed inshore, hopping from headland to headland to avoid the many shipping routes which converge on the canal.

I dived and picked away at the weed-clogged hull many times. It was a bit like mowing a fast growing lawn. As fast as I could scrape away the growth it would reappear. It is a strangely unsettling thing for a single hander to do – to leave the safety of the hull and jump overboard. Even using a buddy line, with the boat stationary and sails lowered, the feeling of vulnerability and loneliness is overwhelming. You stare down into the deep azure blue of the bottomless sea. There is the silence and stillness of inner space familiar to divers. A deep breath through the snorkel and under you go to scrape at an area of hull. With wooden scraper and gloves you struggle with the small, white, razor-sharp barnacles. There are also the larger, bright orange mussels on their long rubbery suckers and the slimy mermaid's hair. The debris floats out below the hull like a cloud of space dust streaming off into the Milky Way. Shoals of fish gather from nowhere to feed in it glinting just at the range of vision. Surely there must be sharks. Is that one over there?

I have never to my knowledge had a close call with a shark, either cleaning the hull or swimming. But often having done some hull cleaning, and regained the safety of the deck, I have seen them lazily swimming about, checking things out.

The gulf of Dulce, Punta Burica and the major island of Coiba slipped by to port. There was much evidence of shipping, both inshore with local craft and offshore with the major shipping lanes. At night *Molly B* would lay ahull, all sails down and an anchor hanging off the bow. I was taking no chances of washing up on another beach. By day I would sail along in the soft breezes intent on picking out the next headland. The frigate birds circled high overhead, the Manta rays broke the surface flying clear like huge bats then landed with a loud crack as they belly flopped into the water. A sea snake slithered by.

To enter the Gulf of Panama on a yacht one is advised to follow the current which sweeps in an anticlockwise direction. So from Punta Mariata I once more stood offshore and crossed the busy shipping lanes to the east side of the Gulf. Then the powerful current took over and flushed *Molly B* to the shining skyscraper city of Panama.

Here was the gateway to the old world, the engineering miracle that is the canal. All I had to do was transit it in the engineless *Molly B*.

# 6

# 'Or Like Stout Cortez . . .'

*'Or like stout Cortez when with eagle eyes*
*He star'd at the Pacific – and all his men*
*Look'd at each other with a wild surmise –*
*Silent, upon a peak in Darien.'*

**M**olly B was anchored off the old city of Panama, a romantic grouping of castellated walls and stone buildings. It lies about a sandy bay that would once have been a safe haven for gold-hauling galleons under the protection of the guns of the port. Now, all that seemed to happen on shore was a busy street market. The stallholders used the bay as a convenient garbage dump for just about everything. Vultures hopped merrily from mountains of vegetable cuttings to carcasses of dead animals. It was possibly the most disgusting place that *Molly B* has ever had to anchor.

A Panamanian gunboat slid up to the anchored *Molly B* and asked me where I was going. I had anchored in an unusual place and also a conspicuous one. I did not want to get involved in Panamanian bureaucracy so indicated that I was heading for the Canal Zone. They

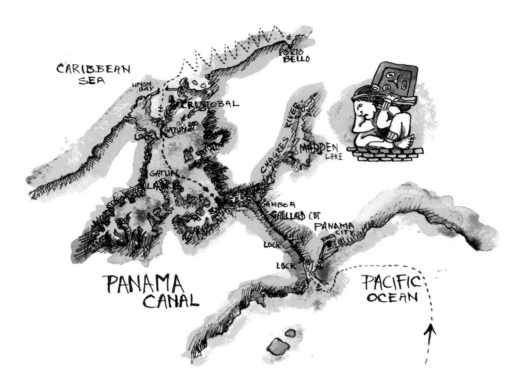

let me go, friendly, as they waved their automatic weapons about nonchalantly in the air.

I upped anchor and sailed to the US-controlled Canal Zone which is a short hop around a breakwater from the city of Panama. Here I anchored at Naos Island among a gaggle of yachts. This anchorage, used by a changing fleet of world cruisers, was home to *Molly B* for the next two months.

I spent a depressing two days messing about with the customs, immigration and secret police in order to clear into the country. I ended up paying a taxi driver to steer and bribe me through the several offices and red tape. Panama, the country and her blushing bride, the Canal Zone, were going through some marital problems. It was difficult to figure out who was in charge of what.

From the early days of the mule trains across the isthmus, to the railroad that joined the two oceans in the 1850s, until the present canal was completed in 1914, Panama has always been an important location. Panama City exists because it is a link between two oceans

and one of the great centres of commerce in the world. The country
of Panama was set up by the US in order to facilitate the building of
the canal. The Canal Zone was effectively US territory until recent
times. In the 1970s Panama as a country had begun to flex its muscles
under the populist leadership of Omar Torrijos. Panama had renegotiated the canal territory lease deal and extracted a promise that the
canal would return to the ownership and control of the Panamanian
people by the year 2000. Torrijos, having stood up to the Americans
and winning the return of the canal, died in a plane crash in 1981.
Now Panama was in the uneasy truce period between the upheavals
of the Torrijos years and the major disruptions which were to char-
acterise the emergence of General Noriega some years later. Many
Americans had left and those who remained were worried. Here and
there about the streets I was to see signs of the recent rioting – burnt
out buildings and cars. The Panamanian army was everywhere. The
US army, though still controlling the Canal Zone, maintained a low
profile. As part of the recently renegotiated canal treaty, wherever a
US employee or US soldier was on duty a Panamanian also had to be
in attendance. In theory, the Panamanian was being trained to take
over the running of the canal.

One of the first casualties of this hand-over treaty, from my point
of view, appeared to be the Panama Canal Yacht Club. Once obviously a well appointed and equipped yacht club used by the American canal employees it had already fallen into the hands of the lo-
cals. They seemed to do nothing all day except make up rules about
what transiting yachts could, and could not, do. All the little things
which cruising yachties like to get up to, such as visiting each other
in their dinghies (you had to use the club launch) to dropping anchor
(moorings only) to having beach parties (no) to hanging up their
laundry in their rigging (absolutely not), were prohibited. The bar
of the club, where everyone congregated, had become a scene from a
Graham Greene novel. Yet another sunny place full of shady, shifty,
spy-type characters on the make.

The only permitted anchorage in the zone was at Naos Island where I had anchored. This was about a one-mile walk from the yacht club. Each day I would walk to the club to check for mail and to read the handy notice board there, which the yachties used.

Another area where the political tensions in the zone worked against the yachties having an easy time was that there was no shopping of any sort for non-canal employees. All shops in the zone were restricted to canal employees or US servicemen. To simply buy a bottle of milk or a loaf of bread was a major difficulty. For me it meant I had to walk for about a mile from the anchorage and then catch a bus the five miles into the suburb of Balboa.

I settled into the anchorage at Naos Island and became good friends with two other long-stay yachts anchored there: *Pantera* and *Wind Chariot*. *Pantera* was a small 28 foot Dufour with Jeff, Cindy and three-year-old Melody on board. They were from the US but the homeport on the back of *Pantera* was proclaimed nebulously as 'Earth'. They had been cruising Central America for several years. Jeff was now working for the Smithsonian Institution, which has a research station in Panama. Having been based in the zone for a year they were full of all the yachting gossip of the canal and the west coast of Central America.

The other friendly neighbour was the 48 foot *Wind Chariot*, a salty looking, aft cabin ketch which Larry and Diane had built in Canada. They had known some of my friends in Vancouver. Larry and Diane were cruising around the world but were on a long-stay halt in Panama while they earned some money chartering their boat. Wind Chariot had all the bells and whistles. On board were a well-equipped workshop, diving equipment, massive aft stateroom and a well-equipped galley. They gave me some salmon which they had canned on board. They even had a TV, which were then just starting to make their appearance on board boats. A huge crowd would congregate on board Wind Chariot for a ball game or a movie.

Everyone I talked to advised me that conditions on the Atlantic side of the canal were much less pleasant than on the Pacific side. The northwest trade winds were still very strong and would remain so for another month. In addition, the city of Colon on the Atlantic side of the canal had a bad reputation for muggers and baddies. Between getting my financial affairs in order, arranging for a tow or a motor to somehow transit the canal and waiting for the northeast trade winds to blow themselves out, I was stuck in the anchorage at Naos Island for a good two months.

Apart from the lack of convenient infrastructure on shore, there were some advantages to the anchorage at Naos Island. There was the world cruising fleet to distract my attention. They were passing through the canal on their annual migration around the globe. They had spent Christmas in the Caribbean islands. Then they had spread their wings and run on the trade winds the 1,500 miles to Panama and transited the canal. On the Pacific side they stopped for last minute preparations and shopping before heading off into the vast reaches of the Pacific. The most common next destination was usually the Marquesas Islands, some 4,000 miles to the southwest.

There were boats of all shapes and sizes in this world cruising fleet. All of them of interest to the dedicated boat watcher such as myself. Here was none of your normal marina fodder, none of the pocket family cruisers which clog up the anchorages and harbours all over the globe and gives yachting a bad name because the boats never go out sailing. Here were boats that were being used. A 25 foot family cruiser, a floating caravan, becomes of interest here because someone is sailing around the world in it. Even more interesting were the specially designed, specially built cruising boats, the greyhounds of the ocean, going places in fine style. All one had to have was money.

I got out my paintbox and easel and went into business as a boat portraitist. Business was brisk. The first few paintings I gave away as I built up a portfolio and got invited for many boat-cooked meals. To other yachts I traded the paintings in the time-honoured tradition of the sea. Bits of old rope, rusty tools, worn out sails and other treasures piled up on the deck of *Molly B*. My best swap I think was a sketch for a copy of the famous admiralty publication *Ocean Passages of the World*. Plus a life ring. Other yachts were happy to pay good hard cash to have their dream ship immortalised.

The nicest part of my picture-touting business was that I met a lot of world cruisers, spending hours swapping tales of travel, adventure and the sea. It was nice to see the interiors of so many cruising boats; these little floating homes which have so much attention lavished on them. A place for everything and everything in its place: equipment, decorations, souvenirs, guns, sextants and galley stoves.

When not painting boat portraits I worked on maintaining *Molly B*. There was a lot to do. The rigging needed a complete overhaul following the slow stressful trip south. In many ways, calm weather is more destructive on the rigging of a sailboat than good strong steady winds.

Jeff from *Pantera* was helping out on another boat called *Sly Boots* and I got roped into helping him. *Sly Boots* was a Maurice Griffith-designed junk-rigged sloop. Her skipper, Dr John Stevens, was one of the most courageous yachtsmen I had ever met. Paralysed almost completely by a stroke and unable to speak, John was sailing his specially-designed, junk-rigged yacht around the world. Having sailed to Panama from England he had transited the canal and set sail for the Marquesas Islands the previous year. Five hundred miles out from Panama, the prop shaft on *Sly Boots* had become disconnected from its motor, slid aft and jammed against the rudder. With a jammed rudder John had sailed in circles for two whole months in an attempt to reach any port. Eventually, an Ecuadorian fishing boat had chanced upon him. It hoisted *Sly Boots* on board and brought John and his boat back to Panama.

There John rested and had the boat repaired. Now, one year later, he was ready to set out again. Jeff and I helped him. We checked out his automatic anchoring system, topped up his fuel and water supply, and did other last minute preparations. John was so disabled that he could not even tie a knot or open a tin. As far as calling for help on the radio he could not even speak, communicating in a series of grunts and head nods. The junk rig he could manage by pulling a series of ropes linked to winches. With much cheering from the other yachts he headed away from Naos Island for his second attempt to reach the Marquesas. Years later I learned that Dr John Stevens and *Sly Boots* had never been seen again, presumably lost at sea.

Uppermost in my mind, obviously, was the problem of getting *Molly B* through the canal. Anyone I spoke to agreed that it should not be too difficult to get a tow through the canal, or to mount a large outboard motor on the stern and power through under my own steam.

I tried advertising for a tow through the canal and asked several powerful looking yachts if they would be interested. None were keen to tow another heavy yacht the 50 miles through the locks and against the wind to the Atlantic. A professional tug answered my ad but I was unwilling to pay the commercial rates which they quoted. I was coming around to the view that *Molly B* would have to transit the canal under her own power.

On board *Molly B* I had a 9.5 HP outboard motor which I had bought from Earnest in Vancouver and had been lugging around ever since. In more optimistic moments I would say, 'No reason why that thing should not get me through the canal.' So I started building a mounting for it.

The mounting of the outboard proved easy. A length of two by two hardwood, a rectangle of thick plywood, four bolts and we were ready to go. I went out for a trial run. The motor seemed to work well in calm seas. The six-ton *Molly B* slowly built up impetus and trundled across the bay at a steady three to four knots. In calm conditions all seemed fine. The 9.5 HP motor whizzed away at full throttle like the egg beater it was. All was fine as long as the prop of the motor remained immersed. However, because the motor was at the very extremity of the hull, any waves caused the prop to jump out of the water as the hull hobby horsed. When that happened, with no resistance against it, the prop raced out of control, the engine making a frightening sound. I felt the engine must explode. Throttle adjustments and gear changes had to be done by the driver leaning long-handed over the side.

It was not an ideal solution, but what the hell. That was the way with the *Molly B*. The question was would *Molly B* be able to motor the 50 miles through the Panama Canal? Would the authorities permit me to make an attempt?

To give the engine further assistance, and because it needed it anyway, I decided to clean and paint the hull of *Molly B*. On the north side of the canal entrance, about two miles from the anchorage, was a long beach which seemed suitable for drying out on the tide. (On one chart which I had on board, a leper colony was marked as nearby but it was said to be no longer occupied.) In a fine display of seamanship, even if I do say so myself, I sailed *Molly B* up on the

beach. It was a tricky situation as a strong current was running like
a river, parallel to the beach. I had to drop two stern anchors and use
two bow lines to control *Molly B* while the tide fell. Two tides were
required to clean and paint the complete hull.

The circus of round-the-world yachts slowed down to a trickle as
the season advanced. The Panamanian spies at the yacht club started
to take an interest in me as I became familiar checking for mail and
reading the notice board. One day I was told I would have to 'renew
my permit'. The trade wind season on the northern side of the canal

drew to its end as the belt of strong headwinds moved south. The work of preparation on *Molly B* progressed well. I became more confident of making the passage through the canal. In short, it was time to move on.

I called the canal authorities and they sent an Ad Measurer, as they are called, to measure the vital statistics of *Molly B*. This is to determine how much the vessel should be charged to transit the canal. It is a cumbersome process that the yacht owner has to pay for. The actual tonnage of the yacht as determined by the canal company measurement system always works out to be quite small. A yacht is treated in the same manner as if it was a 10,000-ton cargo ship. The fees for *Molly B* to transit the canal come to only $50 and most of that was the measurer's fee. More than one transit would be even cheaper as the yacht has to be measured only once. This is now no longer the case and a yacht now transiting the canal can pay around $2,000.

With the underwater hull cleaned, the motor mounted and the measurement certificate granted, all that remained was for *Molly B* to find a crew and book a transit of the canal. Canal regulations require four line handlers to accompany each yacht as it transits on the one-day trip through the canal. The line handlers are necessary to hold the boat against the force of the water surging into the locks as they are filled.

Transiting yachts usually help each other through the canal with crew. Here the single hander is at a disadvantage. Somewhere he has to find at least three other helpers and has only his own services to swap in exchange. Equity would demand that he help three other yachts to get his own yacht through. This I was prepared to do if necessary. At the same time, I was also prepared to hire crew. I was now in funds. Events were to conspire against a normal transit of the canal. Initially, I did a deal with Jim, on the tri *Galatea*, and with a fortunate encounter, one Kristo Babajko on a classic 40' wooden ex-racing boat called *Kuling*. Kristo was to be the saviour of *Molly B*.

I rang the Canal Company and confirmed my transit times. On the morning of St Patrick's Day, March 17th, I headed off with a pilot on board to transit the Panama Canal. Most vessels, in fact all vessels, must complete the 50-mile journey in one day and are not permitted to do otherwise. It was to take *Molly B* three weeks, three pilots, several breakdowns, two tows and much heartache to make the journey.

The day of the transit started early. Jim came aboard followed shortly by the canal pilot, Fred, and we got under way. Two miles up the canal opposite the yacht club we collected Kristo, his girl-friend Marie and Rick, his crew. The morning was calm and the motor pushing well as we headed up the canal, sipping coffee in the early morning sun. No problems as we putted under the giant Balboa Bridge, through busy docklands and canal maintenance depots and into the first of two mighty sets of locks at Miraflores and Pedro Miguel.

The locks themselves proved no problem to the strong crew, stout cleats and nylon ropes of *Molly B*. The drivers of the 'mules', the train engines that move the large ships into and out of the locks, gazed down lazily from the towering walls above. Then they went back to reading their paperback books. They were not interested in the colourful group of adventurers in among the container ships. They had seen it all before.

The locks were the easy part. They required no effort on the part of the motor. We made good time through the first two sets of 'up' locks, Miraflores and Pedro Miguel. 'At least now we are up,' I said to myself as we exited the last of them. 'And what goes up etc etc. We might just as well come down on the Atlantic side as on any other.' But first we had to complete the 40-mile journey across the isthmus.

As the morning progressed, the wind increased from the north as expected. A dead header. The motor whined and strained and pushed us along at full revs. Kristo and the rest of the crew tried not to appear too bored. The pilot, a Panamanian, was businesslike but aloof. He waved to his buddies working on the banks. No one voiced many opinions as to our chances of making it across in one day, but the silence, to me, was ominous. Progress was slow as we battled our way through the famous 8-mile long Galliard cut. Here we start to lose our place in the convoy of ships of which we are a part. The passing ships build up speed in the 500' wide cut. As they hurry past they create a wash. This causes the slow-moving *Molly B* to hobbyhorse. The prop lifts out of the water, spinning at full revs with no resistance from the water, making a frightening whine. The inevitable happens as the racing motor seizes. We drop anchor, let the motor cool down, and get under way again.

The only way to proceed was to reduce revs to reduce the strain on the motor. This reduced hull speed. We were also running out of fuel. I had borrowed as many fuel tanks as possible for the transit, but being unfamiliar with the motor I had no way of knowing how much fuel it would use in 50 miles of motoring. We were going to run out.

At Gamboa, about a third of the way through the canal, pilot Fred made an estimate of our progress and of our chances of getting across Gatun Lake in time to lock down into the Atlantic that day. He called his superiors on his VHF and was instructed to leave the boat at Gamboa for the night. This for me was a disaster. I was keen to press on, having assembled a crew and having got this far. Fuel was apparently available at Gamboa. The Canal Company's instructions were law, however. In addition, I suspected a mini-mutiny behind my back, the crew, anxious to get home for the night, colluding with Fred and the canal controllers. *Molly B* anchored at a small lake in the canal near a maintenance depot. A canal launch removed Fred and the crew. They conveniently caught the trans-Panama railway back to where they had started, leaving me alone on *Molly B*.

There I stayed for two nights, the hot tropical jungle all around, the water full of gambolling manatee, the air full of mosquitoes and other nasty bugs. Probably the same deadly mosquitoes which had held up the building of the canal for so long. I was not short of fresh food however. The crew had jumped ship leaving the supplies for the transit – three roast chickens and a load of other goodies, including a complete watermelon. Without ice to preserve it, I did my best to eat the lot.

Food was the least of my worries. I overhauled the motor as best I could.

The canal authorities gave me special permission to attempt to cross Gatun Lake with only a pilot on board. They must have appreciated the difficulties of raising crew at Gamboa. We headed out and reached the lake, a short distance from Gamboa, around midday. The wind was already blowing to its daily pattern – dead on the nose. All this messing about with toy motors on home-built boats did not amuse the pilot. The wind, a good force 4, was too much for the bulky *Molly B* and the 9.5 HP motor. I tried motor sailing with the mainsail up but it was no use. The pilot shrugged in a resigned sort of gesture as if to say, 'I told you so', and then called up his superiors. We were instructed to return to Gamboa. We turned and flew back with the wind in the opposite direction.

The situation looked a bit grim. Leaving *Molly B* anchored at Gamboa I took the train down to Balboa to help Kristo on *Kuling* through the canal as we had prearranged. Kristo was sympathetic to the plight of *Molly B* when he heard my tale. 'No problem, man,' he said. 'I'll tow you across the lake. You're going to make it Pete.'

Kristo was as good as his word. We set off from Balboa to do the transit of the canal with his classic yacht *Kuling*. This was the sort of yacht the king of Sweden might have had for day sailing. We retraced the steps *Molly B* had taken two days earlier – up through Miraflores and Pedro Miguel locks and through the Galliard Cut. Our pilot talked to the faceless ones who control movements in the canal. They readily gave permission to the *Kuling* to tow *Molly B* through the canal.

Around midday *Kuling* reached the anchored *Molly B*. One of *Kuling's* crew helped me aboard *Molly B* and we got under way. We motored up the cut to the lake and then *Kuling* passed back a towrope. As expected, the afternoon wind was blowing. Gatun Lake, one of the biggest man-made lakes in the world, is the feeder lake for the whole Panama Canal. The route we have to take is 25 miles across before reaching the giant triple locks at Gatun. *Kuling* is a thoroughbred racing boat from an earlier period. Her motor is small and progress is slow. On board *Molly B* we keep the outboard running to help things along. The course across the lake is slightly zig zag so on some legs both *Molly B* and *Kuling* are able to hoist their sails. We must have looked a fine and desperate sight, two motors straining, sails sheeted taut, tacking through the jungle attached by a towrope. I was over the moon, thrilled to be making progress. It looked as if we were going to make it through the Panama Canal. I clung to the tiller straining every last inch out of both motor and mainsail. The tow line was quite long, perhaps 300 feet, so that *Kuling* up ahead was out of shouting range but looked a fine sight as she heeled over under her sails. Sometimes *Molly B* would catch the wind just right and surge ahead. The towrope would go slack and drag in the water as we caught up with *Kuling*. It was like a wonderful race. Kristo would glance behind, give me a clenched fist salute and smile. We were getting there.

The Atlantic was to elude *Molly B* for a little while yet. Progress across the lake was slow for the two boats. *Kuling* was in danger of being late for the last 'down' locking operation of the day at Gatun. Kristo was anxious to get through the canal in one day and be on his way. He had been a great help. The pilot instructed *Molly B* to anchor above the lock at Gatun. *Kuling* cast off the tow, took his crew and hurried on into the mighty locks, which would take them down to the Atlantic level. *Molly B* anchored. In the distance and below, less than ten miles away, I could see the Atlantic Ocean, the ships waiting for transit appearing like dots upon it. It would take another day's work to get there.

The following day I took a train down to Cristobal, the town on the Atlantic side of the canal. I hitched a ferry out to the anchored *Kuling* and thanked Kristo. He was headed back to his native Yugoslavia in the beautiful *Kuling*. From what I could figure out from talking to him, and seeing the way he limped on one of his legs, he had been a biker in California before taking up yachting!

Gatun gives its name to the locks and the lake, and to the pilot station near where *Molly B* was anchored. But there is no town, village shops or residences called Gatun. The Canal Zone is kept squeaky clean in case of a third world war. There I stayed for a further 18 days in sight of the elusive Atlantic. To get to Cristobal involved locking down through the mighty triple locks and then motoring through a cutting for about seven miles to the anchorage at Cristobal. The motor still had a tendency to seize, but having taken *Molly B* this far there seemed every hope that it would take us the rest of the way.

Boats are not normally allowed to stop during a transit of the canal. As usual, things were different for *Molly B*. It was quite pleasant up on the lake in the fresh, soft water. I needed someone to help with the lines during the remainder of the transit. Being cut off from a gaggle of helpful fellow cruisers, this proved a problem. In the end, I hired a lad from the Cristobal Yacht Club.

I was ready to complete the transit. I called the Canal Company and booked my place in the locks. I was allocated a pilot and was impressed when this turned out to be a Captain Jack R. Griffin. *Molly B* got under way and we headed out into the mighty triple lock at Gatun.

Yachts usually draw pilots who are Panamanian and less than a fully qualified Panama Canal pilot. They are even called yacht pilots and are usually off duty tugboat drivers or maintenance employees. The two previous pilots I had drawn had been of this variety. But today I had been allotted a full Panama Canal pilot. Captain Jack R. Griffin was an ex-US navy commander. His wife was from Ireland he proudly informed me. The ropey *Molly B* and the voyage I was undertaking amused him. 'I gotta tell my wife about this,' he said. He was very friendly to me but quite officious with the native line handler who was the other crew.

We had no problem reaching the locks a few hundred yards away under outboard motor. Nor was there much problem locking down through the three giant chambers, each 1,000 feet long and 110 feet wide. There is less strain on ropes and fewer surges in the locks when descending. *Molly B* tied up to the side of a small tug and piggy-backed a ride through the three giant chambers. Captain Jack R. Griffin got into the spirit of things also. He made a big exception for the day that was in it by helping with one of the lines.

*Molly B* passed into the last of the giant lock chambers and slid down into its cavernous depths, the black, oily, dank walls of the lock towering above. Crabs and dark, slimy, creepy crawlies scurried about. Like the start of some Wagnerian opera the giant black gates of the lock open inward. The sleepy mule drivers wave us through,

Captain Jack R. Griffin repeats the order to proceed and *Molly B* chugs slowly out into the harsh salt water of the Atlantic.

The trade winds were blowing straight on the nose and there were seven miles to go. The canal here runs through low-lying mangrove, the channel about 500 feet wide and in places much wider. *Molly B* had sailed out of much tighter corners and could sail the rest of the way if the motor failed. We motored out of the lock and down the fairway. Progress was slow but we were getting there. I was over-joyed once again. Captain Jack R. Griffin was also in good humour. He chatted about the time he had visited Ireland. He pointed out the old abandoned French canal cut leading into the jungle. He checked *Molly B*'s steering compass from a fixed bearing on the chart. Slowly, but reasonably steadily, we made progress.

We were about half way to Cristobal with approximately three miles to go when a passing ship pushed up a big bow wave. Disaster. The prop on the outboard motor popped out of the water once too

often. The motor, straining and whining at full revs, gave off an almighty BANG and stopped, seized solid, never to go again.

I rushed to the bow and dropped the anchor. There was a stiff head wind and we were stopped dead in the middle of the main channel of the Panama Canal. A large car carrier was bearing down on *Molly B* and had to go into reverse. Captain Jack R. Griffin, in decisive military fashion, got on his walkie-talkie and closed down the entire north section of the canal. He was not amused.

I, in my ignorance, was not that concerned. I requested permission to proceed under sail. Captain Jack R. Griffin, who had had enough of picnicking and playing around in small boats, coldly refused. He was busy with his radio giving our position, description and situation. He requested assistance. Possibly seeing his whole reputation in tatters and the laughing stock of the canal pilots, he took a formal stance towards me, the architect of this disaster.

I fiddled with the outboard motor, whipping off the cover. It was kaput. There was a neat hole in the side of the cylinder block and out of it was sticking one of the piston shafts.

Fifteen minutes passed. The traffic in the canal got going again and squeezed past, the amused crews gazing down from the towering superstructures. Captain Jack R. Griffin sternly warned me that this could work out to be expensive for *Molly B*. A fine big rusty canal launch arrived from Cristobal, got a line on board and off we went again.

Half an hour later we were in the anchorage at Cristobal. Captain Jack R. Griffin jumped ship into the launch as quick as he could with his battery of radios. He shouted back as he went, 'It's at the company's convenience'. This took me a while to understand the meaning of. But he did not grin as I promised him a postcard from Ireland.

I was elated. *Molly B* had transited the Panama Canal. A journey which normally takes yachts one day, I had managed to spend 21 days doing. I looked out over the anchorage at Cristobal, what is known as 'The Flats'. It is not a very scenic anchorage but that did not dampen my spirits. I was among the normal gaggle of cruising boats which one finds in a place like Panama. An oil-streaked beach lay to leeward; the breakwaters of the artificial harbour of Limon far off the bow. The busy oil bunkering station of Cristobal lay to starboard, the jungle and the entrance to the canal to port. Over that horizon lay Ireland. Well, sort of. I made a cup of tea, heaved a sigh of relief and hauled out the charts for the Caribbean Sea and the Atlantic Ocean.

# Chapter 7

# 'Hit the Road Jack'

*'Hit the Road Jack, and*
*Don't Ya Come Back No More'*

The wind whistled in the rigging of *Molly B* where she lay to her anchor in the exposed anchorage at Christobal. The north, or Atlantic, side of the canal is quite different in climate and environment from that of the indolent, calm, Pacific side. It is almost the difference between that of the old world and the new. The environment seems harsher, less fresh, the water more polluted, almost tired. The winds are stronger and colder. There are more people, older buildings, more redundant technology. This contrast is noticeable over the 50 mile width of the isthmus. It is a lee shore also, to both wind and current. Boats stop in Christobal for as short a stay as possible. It had once been a beautiful colonial city but was now very run down and lawless.

The next leg of the voyage was across the prevailing winds and with the current, the nascent Gulf Stream as it pushes west and north. *Molly B* had only one option as I saw it – try to make some easting along the coast of Panama and then shoot north, keeping as far as possible off the coast of Honduras which is fringed with many reefs. I would pass west of Cuba and slip into the port of Key West. At least now there would be wind and plenty of it.

I made an early start beating out to the mighty breakwaters that enclose Limon Bay through a huge fleet of waiting, silent, anchored ships. A hard day's sail, short tacking along the shore, reefing and unreefing, brought me to the historic harbour of Portobello.

There I bumped into an old friend from the canal – Clive Kelly and his tri, *Survival*. Clive had tried to make the hop north to Jamaica and had turned back because of heavy seas and headwinds. Not a good omen for *Molly B*.

The following day, I beat on to the east reaching the famous San Blas islands just as the sun was setting. The islands are classic, low, coral keys. Navigation among them must be done by sight-of-eye, picking out the coral heads and shallows by the colour of the water, preferably with the sun high in the sky. With night coming on I was

afraid to attempt the entrance to the lagoon. I tacked back and forth under reduced sail, *Molly B* holding her own in the fading light. I had been on the helm all day. I was tired. I made a quick revision of plans to visit the San Blas islands. I stood offshore to the north across the shipping lanes and sailed as close to the trade winds as possible. Thus I made an unscheduled departure for Florida, some 1,500 miles away.

I did not feel very much in control of the situation. *Molly B* was heading out into a vast river flowing to the west. Downstream in that river were at least 10 low lying islands and cays. It was like a nautical version of Russian roulette.

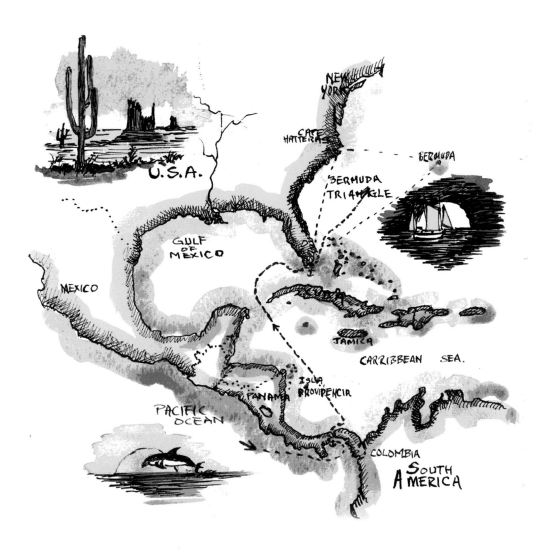

I studied the charts. I must pick up and get a fix on Isla Provedencia, a small island 300 miles to the north, I thought. This would give me the confidence to carry on through the reefs further north.

I ran out the distance and compass course to Provedencia. No island appeared. There was no option but to keep going. To turn back was just as dangerous. Rancador Bank, Seranna Bank, Quito Sueno Bank, Rosalind Bank or Banko Gorda all could have put an end to *Molly B* in a matter of minutes. The current pushed on relentlessly, the trade winds eased off. Four days of very anxious sailing passed. The sun was directly overhead as *Molly B* passed from south to north making it impossible to get a fix. When I finally figured out where we were, just to the south of the tip of Cuba, the danger had passed.

I lashed the helm, went to bed and slept. As dawn broke I stuck my head out of the companionway into the glare of at least four large searchlights. They were beaming down from on high and quite close. A voice was shouting at me through a megaphone. I waved and smiled as I recognised an American accent. 'At least it's not the Cubans,' I thought. I raised the flag in the blinding light. I could just make out the bow of a huge Coast Guard cutter about five yards off the stern of *Molly B*.

The Megaphone wanted to know my name, home port and destination. He told me to turn on my radio. I replied that I had none. I shouted my name. 'HOGAN.' The Megaphone asked me to repeat. 'HOGAN,' I replied and as often with Americans I added, 'SAME AS HOGAN'S HEROES ON THE TV'. There was a bit of a pause and then the Megaphone came back with, 'OK KOJAK, WE'RE GOING TO COME OVER AND INSPECT YOU.'

And so they did. They were looking for drugs. They winched out a launch and motored over the calm sea. Three heavily armed 17-year-olds piled into the cabin of *Molly B*. I had the confidence of someone who knows they have nothing to fear. They shined a torch into the forepeak and looked at my passport and that was that. They were looking for large quantities, obviously. I asked them for a position fix. It turned out to be very close to my estimated position brought forward from the previous day's sights.

Then they were gone. They hoisted their launch up and steamed off over the horizon, a helicopter perched on the stern.

The wind came up from the north east. Just where I wanted to go. With wind against the strong current, the choppy seas made progress difficult. I lay ahull for three days as the current pushed *Molly B* like a bottle into the Gulf of Mexico. This was the start of the Gulf Stream. When things calmed down I was in the middle of a huge fleet of shrimpers. They look very romantic with their huge outriggers. They anchor all day in the shallow Gulf of Mexico and fish all night. They are a nightmare for the singlehanded sailor as they zig and zag about in the dark.

I started to see signs of the coast of Florida to the east – radio stations and the loom of the lights of the city of Naples. We were well to the north of where we should be. I sailed up to a deserted key. Probably Marquesas Key. I never found out. I anchored there for the night and in the morning beat in through the South West channel of the famous harbour of Key West.

It had taken 23 days to sail from Panama, a distance of about 2,000 miles. This was much better progress than in the Pacific, even allowing for the strong current pushing us along all the way. There was a certain amount of luck in it, and luck should play no part in the art of navigation, but I was proud of myself for making the passage from Panama to Key West. I rowed ashore, found a supermarket and loaded up with all the steak, chicken, salad, fresh bread and ice cream I could carry. Then I found the customs and cleared into the good old USA.

I stayed in Key West for nearly two weeks. I found a good local sail maker who did a super job on the sails of *Molly B* which had taken a hiding. He understood the needs of the cruising sailor and the gaff rig and added big rubbing patches on the main sail and the mizzen.

I took it easy in Key West for a few days. I soaked up the sun, fresh food and ice cream. I caught up on sleep and I sat on the beach. Key West is a mellow place and I mellowed out for a while.

Then *Molly B* hopped, in easy stages, the 100 miles up the coast to Miami from where I planned to cast off for my Atlantic crossing. I was looking for a chart agent. There was none to be had, which is surprising for a town the size of Miami. I was told to go to Fort Lauderdale. I needed a chart of the Irish coast. In the end I went into

the Coral Gables Public Library and photocopied a map of Ireland from the Rand McNally atlas which they had. That was my chart for crossing the Atlantic.

I spent the last of my money on anything I thought I might need. A good cushion, winch handle, books, popcorn, powdered cheese cake and chocolate.

'And when our money is all spent
We'll go to sea once more.'

I did not meet anyone in Miami. I simply went about for a week shopping and sightseeing. I rented a bicycle. The night before I departed, a nice girl rowed over from a nearby fishing boat and presented me with a bucket of shrimp. She invited me to dinner the following evening. She said that she and her partner worked on the fishing boat but had a cruising boat. They had been watching me coming and going. I thanked her but said I was leaving to sail across the Atlantic the following morning. And that's what I did.

# Chapter 8

# 'Roll'd to Starboard, Roll'd to Larboard'

*'Roll'd to starboard, roll'd to larboard,*
*when the surge was seething free'*

As if kissing America goodbye, *Molly B* bumped on the ledge off Cape Florida at the exit to Miami. I was trying to cut the corner. The boat bounced a couple of times, came off and kept going. It was a close thing and almost another call for my friends in the Coast Guard.

It was the last day of May. I was setting off to cross the Atlantic at the optimum time – 'by the book'. June and July are the months when there is least chance of encountering a hurricane. I was concerned about the possibility of *Molly B* getting knocked down or worse, capsizing and the ballast shifting. In the bilge were three tons of lead ingots. There was nothing to stop the whole lot going out through the cabin roof in the case of a capsize.

With a light south west wind we stood out into the 50 mile wide expanse of the Gulf Stream as it swishes north. Departing from Miami had the advantage that I could cross the shipping lanes where they are most bunched together and concentrated. I could then hope for a clear run to the north in the shelter of the Bahamas Islands. That was the plan and that was how things worked out.

I steered all night making good boat speed to the north east and making almost as much again in a northerly direction with the help of the current. Twenty-four hours later we were across the Gulf Stream, across the shipping lanes and clear of the keys and reefs to the north of Grand Bahama Island. A fully crewed boat, able to keep a watch for the shipping, would have stayed in the Gulf Stream, riding it to the north for all it was worth. I felt it was better to keep out of the way, using the Bahamas Islands as a sort of shield from the busy traffic lanes.

I was seasick and tired following this overnight effort. I spent the next 24 hours sleeping and neglecting the boat. I felt we were out of danger. The following day, with the first celestial fix of the crossing, *Molly B* was opposite Cape Kennedy, but well to the east. This was an excellent two day run as we were a good 300 miles from Miami. I regained my sea legs, made a huge shrimp curry and settled down for *Molly B*'s first ocean crossing.

If a voyage across the Atlantic can be divided into a beginning, a middle and an end, then this was the end of the beginning. Short and sharp, the Gulf Stream flushed us up into the Bermuda Triangle and away from all dangers. The middle part is the long haul. It comprises the 2,000 odd miles of the Great Circle route of ocean sailing. It runs north, parallel to the coast of the US and Nova Scotia, then out into the cold Labrador Current, across the Grand Banks and east across the north Atlantic. The third and final stage of the journey is the approach to the European continent over the shallower water of the continental shelf which stretches out 700 miles from the land.

The long haul was just beginning. This was my first ocean crossing. *Molly B* performed magnificently compared to how she had performed in the Pacific. It was simply a matter of more wind and, by now, a highly experienced crew.

The first week I reeled off at least 800 miles with a little bit of help from the Gulf Stream. The lack of self-steering was a big disadvantage. It was not the only thing I did not have. No motor, no radio, no lighting, no life lines, no radar, no sounder, no sat nav (GPS did

not then exist), no proper ballast, no crew. It would have been a bit irresponsible to have sought a crew.

But I was happy to be sitting there on the tiller 12 hours a day. I tried self-steering with various rope and pulley methods. *Molly B* would sail upwind and across the wind with the help of some shock cord counterbalancing the tiller. But with the wind anywhere aft of abeam I had to steer. This was what my hero, Eric Hiscock, dubbed 'the tyranny of the tiller'. I ran a line through pulleys into the cabin and so could steer while standing in the companionway. This was handy when rain or heavy weather was happening, when I was cold or when I had to cook in the galley. The galley was right beside the companionway. Countless times during the day I would leave the tiller to put on a sweater, reef a sail or put on the kettle. *Molly B* would slowly curve off course, sails flapping as she pointed head to wind. Her long keel and weight meant that she reacted slowly. I would grab the steering line and pull the tiller up to weather and we would get back on course. It became second nature to me to be connected to my steering line. Like a convict to his ball. It was reason-

ably easy to cook while steering but less easy to navigate. Celestial navigation takes a lot of time and concentration, flustering about with time signals, tables, sums and plotting sheets. While I did this three times a day *Molly B* would lay ahull, sails flapping.

At night I went to bed. Depending on the direction of the wind I adjusted the sails and the tiller. Sometimes I simply had to drop sails and drift downwind.

The second week of the crossing we logged 676 miles. The third week we did slightly better, just short of the magic 700 miles. This was about the half way stage. Here *Molly B* crossed the New York to Cape Town shipping lanes. Like crossing a highway in the ocean it was marked by much flotsam. *Molly B* passed close enough to the Greek tanker *Michael* to read the name on its stern.

My celestial navigation was finally spot on. Maths was never my strong subject. Using the sextant, the sun, US navy tables, a cheap transistor radio and piece of graph paper I was able to accurately calculate our course across the ocean. Taking a fix three times a day, the lines on the chart intersect. A bad result reveals

itself and the smooth course plotted on the chart increases in ac-
curacy as the voyage progresses. It's a time-consuming business but
that is why the navigator was the most important person on board.
That has been the way since the Phoenicians. Now Sat Nav existed
and GPS was being developed. But I had none of that. I did have a
Walker traffrail log, a spinning propeller over the stern which gave
me a reading of distance travelled.

I spent many hours on the tiller. There was no other way. The
weather was still quite warm as we headed north. I read and did rope
work, sewing and repairing, while I steered. The steering became
second nature to me. I could tell we were on course by the motion,
the wind or sun in my face or the flapping of the sails. Whether on
deck or below, dozing or reading, cooking or navigating, I could tell
if we were on course and sailing OK.

The fourth week out from Miami, *Molly B* achieved the hoped for
700 miles for seven days. The cold Labrador Current appeared, its
green icy water contrasting with the azure blue of the Gulf Stream.

We were 400 miles south of St John's in Newfoundland. Fog and mist descended covering everything in a blanket of cold dew. Further north there was the danger of ice. I saw lots of fishing gear on the Labrador Banks – tall, sentinel like, bamboos sticking out of anchored buoys. Longliners.

And then the voyage nearly ended. I fell overboard. I was washing my teeth at the mizzen rigging. The boat gave a lurch in the

choppy sea and over I went. I caught the mizzen rigging and a rope lying there. I clung to the gunnel, my bottom half trailing in the water. With an almighty heave I hauled myself back on board. I was very shook up. It was cold also. That might have been the end of the line. Literally.

I lit the stove, ignored the sailing and had a hot chocolate and a post mortem. From now on 'safety first'.

In these cold foggy conditions the wood burning stove, made in the famous foundry in Lunenburg Nova Scotia, just over the horizon, came into its own. Without it I think I would have had great difficulty getting out of my sleeping bag. I had lots of firewood, gathered from the beaches of Central America. Fine hardwoods. In the oven of the tiny stove I baked potatoes and bread. Here is my recipe for bread:

Half cup thick powdered milk
1 cup flour
1 cup oatmeal
Pinch baking soda
Pinch sugar
Pinch salt
Pinch pancake mix
Squirt of cooking oil
Some raisins
Some chopped coconut
One egg.
Mix the lot and leave in oven for about an hour.

I sat freezing on the helm. I wrapped myself in a big army surplus coat, two pairs of pants, oilskins and wellies. There were birds following all the way across the Atlantic. I could never figure out if they were the same birds all the time or if they changed. They stayed ahead of *Molly B* dipping close to the water. Perhaps the movement of the hull disturbed the fish which they pounced upon.

A storm passed through. *Molly B* recorded her best day's run of 128 miles, noon to noon, and then I had to take in all sail and lie ahull for a day. Everything was fresh, tight, exciting, and there was wind to throw away. Hour after hour sitting by the tiller in the waves or standing in the companionway, the steering rope in my hand, I was getting there.

At the start of the sixth week *Molly B* had logged 3,283 miles from Miami. I was getting indications that the end was in sight. First, I met some warships. Sleek grey presences on the horizon. Perhaps they were the same ones who picked up my buddy Enda as he drifted across the Atlantic in a rubber dinghy. The cold war was still on. Perhaps they tried to talk to me, but they kept their distance. Then I heard the sonic booms from Concorde as it sped across to New York. The number and variety of birds increased – gannets which are supposed to go home at night. Then I heard the news from Radio Éireann! The bus drivers in Phibsboro were on unofficial strike! It was difficult for northsiders to get to work.

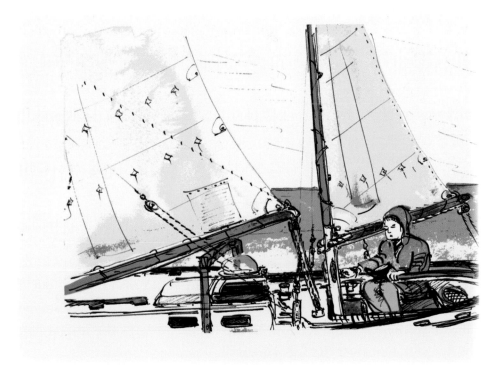

The end was near. I started cleaning up on board. Smelly socks and mildewed underwear got stowed away out of sight. I hauled out the anchor and chain. I found some flags. I cleaned the galley.

Navigation becomes a constant concern. I have my atlas page from the library. I use this to construct a plotting sheet on which the actual celestial navigation takes place. I spend hours scanning the horizon. Small inshore trawlers, of the type I used to work on, appear here and there, but not near enough to hail.

Then early in the morning, LAND AHOY. At first I thought it was the Aran Islands. Then all the islands joined up and I guessed that I was looking at the Cliffs of Moher and Loop Head with its distinctive light house. I was 20 miles to the south of where I had hoped to be. I turned north and reached along the famous Cliffs of Moher on the coast of County Clare.

I followed the local fishing boats into the harbour of Kilronan in the Aran Islands which I knew to be a good, safe anchorage.

It had taken *Molly B* 44 days to sail from Miami. I dropped anchor. Almost immediately local yachtsman Mike Clark from Galway came on board and invited me for a meal on his Dufour 34. It was good to talk to Mike and his crew and eat an Irish stew full of fresh vegetables. They gave me a chart of Galway Bay and dropped me back on board to sleep a long, contented, anchored sleep.

A few days later Dad arrived over from Dublin to congratulate me. He took me up to the nice hotel in Carraroe for a slap up meal. I felt like the prodigal son. 'Why don't you try Brazil or Australia?' he said.

# Chapter 9

# 'Take a Walk on the Wild Side'

*'Hey Babe,*
*Take a Walk on the Wild Side*
*Said Hey Honey*
*Take a Walk on the Wild Side'*

I sailed *Molly B* north to Achill, a stormy, rocky, boggy, mountainous island in the county of Mayo. There, in Achill Sound, beside the Pirate Queen's castle, I stored *Molly B*. I stayed in the west of Ireland for a winter. I attempted to become a famous artist, an Irish amalgam of Paul Gauguin, James Joyce and Andy Warhol, all rolled into one. Well, that did not happen.

In the spring I overhauled *Molly B*. I sailed around Ireland the following summer. Then I located *Molly B* and myself in Dublin. There *Molly B* stayed for the next few years. In the summer *Molly B* would moor in the harbour at Dun Laoghaire. For the winter I would bring *Molly B* up the Liffey and take shelter in the river or retreat into the Grand Canal dock nearby. There, during that period, before the mad property boom arrived, a thriving marine community was developing on vacant land around the old canal basin.

I bought a house on the banks of the Liffey, though far up river, in the little village of Lucan. I slowly resumed the building of *Molly*

B, upgrading and improving her equipment from the basic hull in which I had sailed from Vancouver. I got new, heavier, masts from the Irish forestry service in Wicklow. New rigging from the famous Snatcher rigger in Dun Laoghaire. Lifelines and pulpits. I encased the three tons of lead in *Molly B*'s bilges in cement. Finally, with the help of a French boat builder friend, I installed a motor in *Molly B*, a fine 18 HP Volvo. This motor allowed me to have all kinds of electrical gismos – navigation lights, a radio, and a GPS.

I sailed up to Scotland on a short cruise. On another cruise I almost ran up on the north coast of Cornwall in the fog. With the new motor I spent a winter ascending the Shannon River as far as Lanesborough, passing through Limerick city and the power station there.

I worked hard, opening an art gallery, selling pictures to tourists. The lease on the gallery ran out after three years and I could not renew it. I had money in the bank, a small house, no family and no other commitments. I decided to sail around the world.

*Molly B* was as ready as she would ever be. I got new sails, charts, books. I sent off to California for a self-steering vane. I bought a life raft, stove, and spares for everything.

My old Dad fell ill with cancer. He was 85 years old. I went and visited him in hospital. The doctors thought he would live another two years. I told him I was going to sail around the world. I don't think he heard me. He never listened to me. Now, he certainly had other things on his mind.

I spent the summer preparing. It was October, late in the season. My sister Felicity and her friends gave me a great send-off in a restaurant in Dun Laoghaire. They filled up the boat with wine and fruitcake. It was a windy autumn night. They dropped me at my dinghy late that night after the restaurant and I rowed out in the rain to the waiting *Molly B*. I lit a fire in the stove and crashed out, still moored in the harbour.

I awoke in the morning a little worse for wear. The wind was blowing a gale, but it was from the north. I was heading south. The boats on their moorings in the harbour looked forlorn and wind-swept. I made a slow start under small jib and reefed mizzen. The motor could barely push the heavy hull out of the harbour into the wind. There was no one on the grey pier to wave good bye.

*Molly B* turned around the curve of the pier, the sails filled and off we whizzed across Scotsman's Bay and through Dalkey Sound. I was well wrapped up in woollies and oil skins. Passing Coleimore harbour, there on the quay a figure was waving. My sister Clare and her daughter Moselle were following me down the coast in their car.

I got the self-steering working as we flew across Killiney Bay. I grabbed a bucket and puked my guts out. Then I felt a bit better. The new self-steering worked like magic. I stood in the companionway and watched the coastline speed by. The GPS gave me our speed. We were doing 9 knots as we rounded Wicklow Head on a favour-able tide. Approaching the Arklow Banks I jibed out into the middle of the Irish Sea. 'Good bye Ireland,' I said, as it disappeared in the mist. I did not see the powerful Tuskar light as we sped past. I felt a

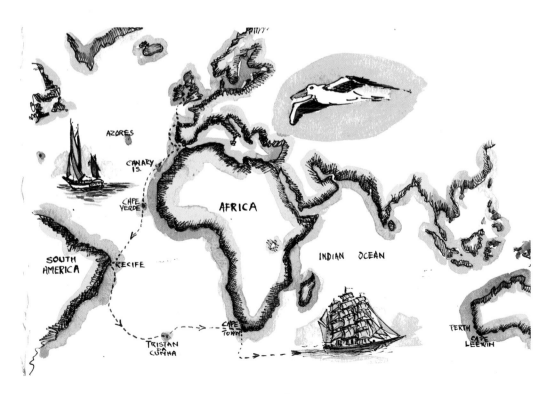

bit like a German battleship breaking out of the Baltic into the North Sea. October is not the best time to cross the Bay of Biscay. There is no best time to cross the English Channel, perhaps the busiest shipping corridor in the world. *Molly B* sped onward in the northerly gale.

Forty-eight hours after leaving Dublin, the Scilly Isles were abeam as *Molly B* flew on. I stayed up the following night crossing the busy shipping lanes, plotting the tracks of the passing shipping. The wind increased, we were across the shipping lanes, and I dropped all sail and lay ahull for a day. Then under a storm jib I sailed west for a further 12 hours.

To my horror I realised I had left the navigation lights on. The batteries were dead. I tried starting the motor by hand. No go. As the wind eased I drifted into the Bay of Ferrol and tied up in the beautiful harbour of La Coruña on the north west tip of Spain. The yacht club there quickly put the batteries on charge for the night while I wandered around the old town. There is a big fishing fleet working out of La Coruña and the many ship chandlers nearby found me stocking up on fish hooks and charts.

My luck held with the weather. Four days after arriving I motored out of the harbour of La Coruña and hoisted sails in the northeast wind. The shipping lanes bunch together as they round the northwest corner of Spain. I spent another anxious night as *Molly B* reached out to the west, well offshore and away from the shipping.

I stopped in Gibraltar. It was a mistake. I thought the shopping would be good. In the end I bought a large quantity of orange juice but little else. I wandered about the marinas and apartment developments, read the notice boards, spoke to the odd yacht owner. I looked at the sun-bleached cruising boats. I felt a bit out of place. *Molly B* with her solid wooden masts and bucket for a toilet did not seem to fit in either. Shopping trolleys full of duty free drink were rolled down the marina jetty by beautiful, healthy looking, girl crews. All was stowed aboard by beautiful, healthy looking, boy crews. Gen-

erators hummed all night powering TV sets, microwaves and air conditioning units. At the end of the jetty close to *Molly B*, in pride of place, was a large motor yacht called *Lady Ghislaine*, owned apparently by Robert Maxwell.

I decided that the Mediterranean and the Suez Canal was not for me. Better to head off into the wide open spaces of the southern ocean. Just 100 years earlier, in August 1895, Joshua Slocum in Gibraltar had made the same decision. He headed south to struggle with the Straights of Magellan. I headed south to struggle with the roaring forties.

I bought some charts and set off back out through the Straits of Gibraltar passing close to the Bay of Tangiers. The course for the Canary Islands runs parallel to the desert for most of its length. The hot spicy smell of the desert comes wafting off the land on the light winds. I turned on the BBC World Service to hear that Robert Maxwell had been drowned off his yacht, the *Lady Ghislaine*, in the Canary Islands.

I dropped anchor in Los Cristianos on Tenerife. Someone had recommended it. It is a local fishing harbour and does not have a marina, both plusses in my book. I spent a pleasant few days shopping, sitting in the sun, eating hamburgers, peeping at topless ladies on the beach and visiting other boats. I was starting to get into the rhythm of being king of the road, master of the waves, and a hard man of the sea.

One day I lifted up the payphone in the town square and in a few seconds was talking to Dad in Dublin. He was convalescing at home and was not that impressed to hear from his wandering son. I said good bye.

It was from the Canary Islands that Columbus set sail, and many other voyagers down the centuries. Now the Atlantic Rally for Cruisers was gathering. *Molly B* stocked up on diesel, eggs and oranges. In the morning I set sail.

I immediately picked up the famous northeast trade winds, some-times known as the Portuguese trades. I was heading south across the winds, perfect conditions for *Molly B* to eat up the miles. Three days out from Los Cristianos I clocked up 153 miles in a noon to noon run. This record was to stand until *Molly B* was close to Cape Horn in the roaring forties.

The wonderful thing about trade winds is that they do not vary in strength or direction for days and weeks on end, unlike the winds in higher latitudes. The sun heats up the surface of the earth at the equator. The hot air rises. The surrounding air to north and south rushes in to fill the space vacated by the rising air. The earth revolving on its axis nudges this moving air to the side and it be-comes a trade wind. All over the world yachts raise their sails and speed downwind using this unlimited free source of power. This was why Columbus discovered America and why in Brazil they speak Portuguese.

With self-steering and GPS, life was magic. I dropped anchor in the Cape Verde Islands eight days later. Immediately *Molly B* was covered by a swarm of little boys who swam, rowed and scurried out from shore. Black shiny bodies, wide clear eyes, fuzzy hair and smiling faces, they demanded to be my agent.

The harbour was crowded with cruising boats and old steam tugs. Ashore I have difficulty buying rotting onions and dirty paraffin. Forget about anything else. The shops are full of tins of oil marked

1967 he was met by a huge welcoming flotilla. His boat, *Gipsy Moth 4*, was hauled out and he did any amount of alterations to it. The Queen knighted him. He was feted, wined and dined and he sailed on again hailed by another flotilla. Nowadays those who go a sailing have to pay their way.

There was a pile of letters for me at the yacht club, plus a small note on the notice board:

'For Peter Hogan. *Molly B* – Pl's phone Micaela.'

Australia is known as the lucky country. I called Micaela and she arrived down to Rushcutters Bay on Saturday morning to 'see the boat'. She was the friend of a friend of my sister Felicity. She had done some sailing, mostly in the Caribbean. 'I like to be on the water' is one of her bons mots. I don't think she was that impressed with the cabin of the 30 foot long *Molly B*. 'Where's the bed?' she asked, eyeing the forepeak full of buckets and sails. She was sitting on the bed. 'Ill show you later,' I winked.

We went for a sail out on the harbour and watched the start of a big ocean race. We did a tour of the local landmarks. That evening we went to her favourite Spanish restaurant – Capitan Torres – on Liverpool Street. Then we saw a flamenco performance. Then I walked her home.

*Molly B* was safely moored in Ruscutters Bay but I had run up on the rocks of true love. Micaela worked during the day as a Montessori teacher. An Irish mother and American dad had produced an exotic mix. A great linguist, she had many friends, particularly in the Mexican/Spanish community of Sydney. She had arrived in Australia five years earlier and liked the easy going sun-filled, laid back lifestyle. There was always something to do, a party, a concert, an exhibition or a BBQ. She introduced me to chorizo and tapas. We sat around on street side cafes watching the people go by. We shopped at the weekend markets. We went to the beach, to movies, swimming pools, galleries and restaurants. We took ferries round the harbour and buses out into the bush. *Molly B* lay forgotten in Rushcutters Bay.

Recife was a horrible place. I was anchored in a commercial harbour on a river. The river was filthy, the colour of coffee or perhaps Guinness. On one side was a busy working port, on the other a shanty town. The anchorage was the sewer for the shanty town. There were no other yachts. Always a bad sign.

I had little luck in Recife. I got ripped off by a taxi driver and bothered by an endless stream of people offering to help me, look after the boat or offering me fire water. I began to feel that the boat and its contents might be a bit vulnerable to a cut-throat gang. I ran for it. I bought a pineapple for 10,000 cruzeiros and still don't know if it was worth it. Without being able to take on water or much fresh food I sailed away from smelly Recife.

I headed south past a huge, rusting, anchored ship which had been burnt out. A super tanker once, it was now a post modern floating island like something out of *Waterworld*. It was occupied by smiling faces, all fishing over the side. The biggest house boat in the world. I waved and kept going.

I passed the Brazilian island of Trindade. The vast area of the South Atlantic opened out before me, fresh and full of sea life. Virtually empty of shipping. Whales gambolled and breached before me. The sun reigned supreme in a cobalt sky over an azure sea. In the moonlight the plankton in the water shines like the Milky Way. Flying fish land on deck and flap in the scuppers. Dolphins dart across the bows. Sailfish belly flop lazily nearby. The mahi mahi dart about in a flash of silver. These were the horse latitudes.

Then we entered the westerlies and *Molly B* sped off to the south east dropping anchor in the deep water off the most remote inhabited island in the world – Tristan da Cuna. I had trouble finding it in the misty conditions and using the map in my *Times Atlas of the World*. The magic GPS told me I was 17 miles away from the high volcanic island. Still I could not see it. Then it appeared out of the mist.

I had difficulty anchoring in the deep water. I spoke to the island on the VHF. I was told the harbour was closed until the weather improved. I waited over night and then rowed ashore through the surf on to the black volcanic beach. As if in warning the beach was littered with the wreck of a fine 40 foot yacht. I walked over the fields towards the village of Edinburgh. Two people approached me and explained that they were the police from the island. They told me to return to my yacht and that what I had done was very foolhardy. 'You must wait till the harbour is open. You could be blown away in your dinghy,' they say. They were right. I returned to *Molly B*. If I had lost an oar or even an oarlock I would have been blown out to sea.

The Administrator of the island came on the radio and read me the riot act. He said I must wait. I think he was sensitive that the

island might be invaded like the sister Falkland Islands had been not so long ago. Having made a token landing, I decided to call it quits. I hauled up the anchor from the deep, a haystack-sized load of seaweed fouling it. I hacked away at the seaweed with a bread knife. I waved good bye to the misty isle and headed for South Africa.

I was running low on water, fresh food and diesel for the motor, not having had a good shop or filled the tanks since the Canary Islands. But there was lots of wind. The albatross glided about the horizon and in the colder waters I started to catch tuna. As I approached Cape Town I passed many fishing boats and a diamond drilling rig, not unlike an oil rig. As I approached the harbour it was getting dark. There was a handy island on the chart called Robben Island. For a while I considered anchoring in its lee for the night. Lucky I did not. It is a high security prison. I might have been blown out of the water. I pressed on into the well lit harbour of Cape Town. Traffic control came on the radio. They were surprised to find me within their walls. They directed me to the yacht basin. I tied *Molly B* up, ate the last of the biscuits and breathed a sigh of relief.

# Chapter 10

# 'Nkosi, Sikelel' iAfrika'

The white apartheid regime was still in control in South Africa while I was there. Things were a bit tense. Talks were taking place as to the best way to set up a new constitution for the country.

I went and checked in at the Royal Cape Town Yacht Club. They are a highly efficient, famous old outfit. In no time at all they had assigned me a space, helped me move to it, exchanged some money for me, sent off some faxes for me, informed customs and immigration that I was here and showered and fed me. They warned me about going up town after dark. Customs and excise arrived wearing the colonial rig of white knee socks and shorts which I associate with South Africa. They processed me quickly and without fuss. 'Stay as long as you like, Captain,' they said and scurried off.

The docks area was a mixture of a well run, restricted, port complex and total confusion. The vast area was fenced off from the town and blacks were restricted from entering. Armed guards stood watch on the yacht club 24/7. An old section of the busy port was being developed into a dining/tourist/recreation area. Huge bulk carriers landed raw grain for the starving masses reported to be in Zimbabwe. People slept in rubbish skips. Taxis delivered girls down to the ships and waited round for them. There were bars, music, fork lift trucks and dirt everywhere. Beyond the fence was the no go area of Woodstock, beyond that was the bulk of Groote Schuur Hospital, famous for the first heart transplant, beyond that the iconic shape of Table Mountain.

I made friends with Alan who lived in the marina. He drove me around and knew everything there was to know about Cape Town and sailing. He even knew where Bernard Moitessier had stayed when he had passed through Cape Town on his first voyage. Moitessier had used the frayed ropes from the whalers to weave new ropes for his own *Marie-Thérèse*. He had lived on cormorants, shot with his sling. He also had a fondness for dog biscuits.

Alan and his friends were creationists and argued long and hard with me that the Bible was correct and that God had created the world in six days. But we did not fall out over it. I was in good company. Joshua Slocum also met a member of the Flat Earth Society when in South Africa and had to explain diplomatically that he was sailing round the world.

*Molly B* was looking a bit the worse for wear. I resisted the temptation to haul out in Cape Town. But I gave the boat and its equipment a good going over. I found a sail maker to patch up the sails. I dived on the hull in the filthy harbour and scraped it. I stocked up on the excellent local produce. Biltong is a local delicacy – tough dried meat invented by the Boers. It was not a great success. I bought a concertina thinking I might teach myself how to play it. I sent off faxes to my dad. He seemed happier that I had made it this far and his buddies in the yacht club bar were following my progress. I was in a shop one day when an argument started between two customers. One of them pulled back his coat to reveal a neat pistol in a holster in the style of Dodge City! Cape Town was a city of deep contrasts. Many white South African people I spoke to were curious about where in the world they could move to and how could they take their money with them. They asked about buying a boat. I decided South Africa was not the place to stop.

The sailing directions in my trusty *Ocean Passages for the World* were very specific about how to proceed from Cape Town in a vessel under sail. '*Stand boldly to the southwest until the westerly winds are reached or the wind changes to a more favourable direction. Steer nothing east of south so as to avoid the area southeast of the tail of the Agulhas bank where gales are frequent and heavy and dangerous breaking seas prevail.*' Again I stayed up all night to keep watch in the shipping lanes. I encountered the largest shoal of dolphin I have ever seen. You could have walked across the sea on the back of surfing dolphins. If only I could have harnessed a few hundred of them.

I had great difficulty sailing south from Cape Town in search of the westerly winds. It was not until I reached the famous 40th parallel and had been pushed well to the west that the winds picked up and we made some progress. Again, the recommended route is along the 40th parallel with warnings to keep a good look out for icebergs. I did not find any.

It was eight days before *Molly B* encountered the strong westerly winds she was seeking and I could point the bow to the east. This is the route of the old square riggers, 'running down their easting' in the roaring forties.

The pattern of westerly winds, interspersed with a day or two of calms accompanied by lumpy seas, repeated itself again and again as the weather systems moved around the world unimpeded. *Molly B* made good progress when the winds blew. But it was slow going for the heavy hull, combined with the gaff rig and small sail area in the periods in between the westerlies. It became a matter of waiting patiently for the sea to calm down and the wind to pick up. Lying on my bunk below I feel the first stirrings of the waves as they organised themselves into a pattern. The slapping of the sails and the banging of the spars up above slows down and ceases. The motion becomes steady; the hull gently leans over to one side. The sea hisses as it slips by. I go on deck. I adjust a few of the sails, clear the coffee cups and books from the cockpit. I adjust the self-steerer. I scan the horizon. No ships, no icebergs. I retire below. I make a log entry. We are off again. The sea is calm while the wind increases so *Molly B* glides along.

The wind builds up steadily over the hours. The water rushes by the hull. I cook. I eat. I sleep. I listen to the radio – Alistair Cooke's *Letter from America* or *Desert Island Discs*. As the wind strength builds up I reduce sail. From genoa to jib. Then two reefs in the main. Then drop the main completely. Then a reef in the mizzen. Finally, if necessary, a storm jib and drop the mizzen. The entire cycle usually lasts for about four days as the wind system passes through and the pattern repeats itself.

South of the 40th parallel it can be a bit cold. I am glad to have the wood stove. The cabin stays warm and dry. The kettle simmers away on the hob. It had been difficult to get firewood in Cape Town. The local poor people cook on open fires. Every week or so I force myself to take a bath. I go up on the foredeck with bucket and Fairy Liquid. I trail a rope astern in case I fall or trip. I wash in the sea water, a good scrub all over. Fairy Liquid dish washing stuff works better than soap in the salt water. Then I slosh at least three buckets of good clean refreshing Indian Ocean, roaring forties, water over my head. More if I can stand it. Then I finish off with about a half bucket of fresh water to wash away the salt. Back down into the

cabin to the waiting stove to dry off. All the while *Molly B* ploughs steadily to the east at her regal speed of 5 miles per hour.

It was not until 34 days out from Cape Town that I managed to catch the first and only fish of the crossing. A very welcome blue fin tuna. It was a big fish. I logged my meals for the period that it lasted:

*Friday:*

Dinner: Fried fresh tuna, beans, beer, coffee, biscuit.

*Saturday:*

Breakfast: Fried tuna, cocoa, crackers, jam.
Lunch: Fried tuna, pickles, cocoa, Turkish delight.
Dinner: Fried tuna boiled potatoes, ketchup, beer, cocoa, and biscuit.

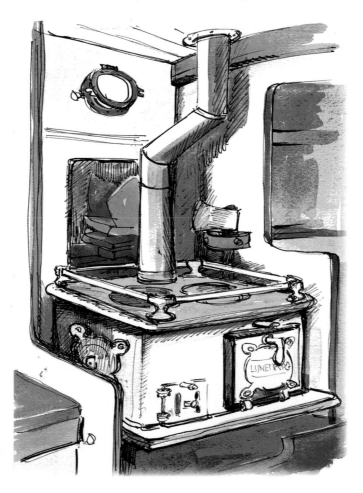

*Sunday:*

Breakfast: Cocoa, granola, grapefruit juice.
Lunch: Fried tuna, fried potatoes, ketchup, coffee, biscuit.
Dinner: Curried tuna, fried potatoes, fanta, chocolate bar.

*Monday:*

Breakfast: Grapefruit juice, cocoa, crackers, jam, dried prunes.
Lunch: Fried tuna, crisps, wine, coffee, dried fruit.
Dinner: Curried tuna, rice, tinned asparagus, wine, coffee, chocolate.

*Tuesday:*

Breakfast: Juice, coffee, pancakes.
Lunch: Fried tuna, asparagus, rice salad, cocoa, biscuit.
Dinner: Fried tuna, fried rice, cocoa.

And then the fish started to rot and I threw the rest overboard.

I passed close to St Paul's Island, about midway across the Indian Ocean. Unfortunately, I did not see it. It is the tip of an extinct volcano and boats can sail into the crater. *Molly B* passed by at night and in heavy weather. It was an important way point in the days of the clipper ships and would have made an interesting short stop. I called out into the night on the VHF but there was no reply.

As *Molly B* approached the Australian continent I eased up to the north out of the forties heading for Freemantle. The final few days were marked by squally wet weather. Then the water colour changed to a beautiful deep azure – the warm current which flows south along the west coast of Australia. I picked up the light off Rottnest Island, 55 days after leaving Cape Town. This was the longest hop to date which *Molly B* has made. It was a slow passage because of the delay getting south at the start of the trip. The harbour master came out from the marina to meet me in a fine launch. He led me straight to a berth in front of the Freemantle Yacht Club where I was greeted by the four divisions of officialdom. They were the Australian customs, excise, police, and quarantine complete with sniffer dogs. I think they were expecting trouble.

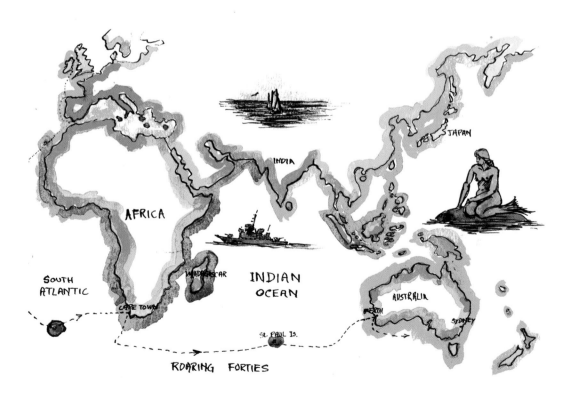

# Chapter 11

# 'Waltzing Matilda, Waltzing Matilda'

*'Waltzing Matilda, Waltzing Matilda*
*You'll come a-Waltzing Matilda with me'*

The Aussie authorities were convinced that I was not what I appeared to be. They turned the boat upside down looking for drugs or something. They did not believe that I had sailed from Cape Town. They thought I was an illegal immigrant. They threatened to rip the boat apart searching it. They took what food was left on board, which was not much, and presumably burned it. Then they insisted I deposit a load of money in a bank account and welcomed me to Australia.

And it turned out to be a great place. The best marina in the world, the best boatyard in the world, the best yacht club dining room in the world and the friendliest people in the world. I am surprised I am not still there. *Molly B* was parked next door to Lin and Larry Pardey, the best sailing couple in the world on their engineless *Taleisin*. I had some of their books on board. They are the natural successors to Susan and Eric Hiscock in the pantheon of cruising greats.

I bought a bike in a jumble sale. One needs wheels in a place like Australia. It's a bit like California that way. I hauled *Molly B* out of the water in the yard and set to work cleaning her up. The boat yard and marina had been built to accommodate the now departed America's Cup where Alan Bond had lost the Cup back to the Americans. Now, there was lots of spare space for *Molly B* and the Australians were preparing to throw Bond into prison.

Dad, to my surprise, jumped on a plane and came and visited me for four days. All of a sudden I was persona grata and a hero. He enjoyed his visit then flew back to Dublin to tell his buddies in the yacht club that all was well.

I met a girl! Helena was 26 years old. She had a daughter aged 13. She had another one aged 6. We sailed out to Rottnest Island for a date. I asked her if either of the fathers of her children had ever contributed to their maintenance. 'One of them once gave me $60,' she replied. I thought it was a particularly Australian story.

I got friendly with Ian and his girlfriend Coleen. We went out fishing with his dad. His mum was an expert on gold. They took me out into the bush looking for kangaroos. The only kangaroos I saw were in a compound for the tourists at Perth International Airport.

I was keen to keep moving on. I wanted to see some more of Australia and get across the Great Australian Bight before winter set in. People seemed genuinely sorry to see me go. Freo is a small town as is Perth a small city when compared to the vast open spaces of Western Australia, a state the size of Europe with a population of four million.

I left Freo in the morning and got a good run to the south around famous Cape Leeuwin. The wind was off the land and so the seas

were flat and the wind eases as *Molly B* rounds the south west corner of Australia. It is 1,380 miles to Bass Strait. I have been advised to get back down south into the roaring forties again, well offshore. This I do but the Bight lives up to its reputation as one of the stormiest places in the world as the huge rollers from the south pile up into the shallow waters of the Bight.

*Molly B* was soon down to her shortest sail combination, a storm jib and a reefed mizzen, but we were still screaming along, making over 130 miles a day. Occasionally a big roller would scream up from behind breaking just at the wrong time and spew *Molly B* around broadside on. The tiny cockpit would fill and the wave crash over the cabin. But the magic self-steerer would regain control hauling the tiller up to windward and off we would go on course again. There

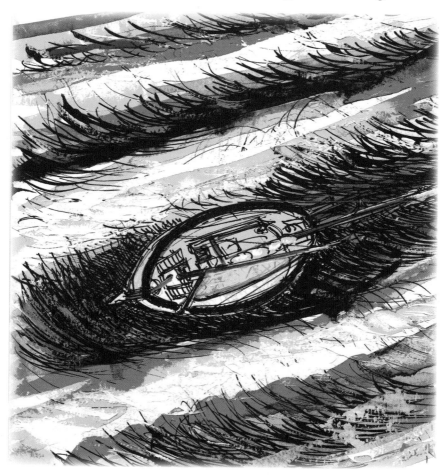

was not much I could do. I knew that we were at some sort of limit. I just had to keep calm and hope that the masts and other gear held. After three days of this breakneck pace *Molly B* suffered a knock down. We were on the port tack so I was on the starboard bunk. Suddenly there was a whoosh like the sound of a breaking wave on a beach, then an almighty BANG as the breaking wave hit *Molly B*. All the books from the port side rained down on me. The contents of the galley ended up on the chart table. A bit like a swing boat in a fun fair, *Molly B* rights herself. On deck the masts were still standing and the sails intact. One of the lifeline stanchions had been broken and the others bent where a dodger was attached to them. We continued on. At noon that day *Molly B* clocked up a further 139 miles which included the knock down. We were screaming along like an overweight surfer, out of control.

I decided to stay away from the shallow water of Bass Strait. I headed for the safety of Portland, a deepwater port offering good shelter.

It was a holiday weekend in Australia. The Queen's birthday, I think. Portland is the site of the first white settlement in the state of Victoria, dating from 1833 when a farmer rowed his cattle across Bass Straight from Tasmania and started farming. His first, hand-held plough is preserved in the little museum there. Twenty years later gold was to be discovered in the mountains of Victoria and the ensuing gold rush is effectively the start of modern Australia.

*Molly B* pressed on and entered Port Phillip Bay through the rip at its entrance where tides run at six knots. You have to go through at slack water. I sailed across the bay and stayed in Melbourne for a month, enjoying possibly the nicest and most civilized of the Australian cities. I tied up in the old abandoned docks area. There, I befriended a bunch of sailors and boat builders who helped me repair *Molly B* following her pasting in the Bight. Both Conor O'Brien and Joshua Slocum had made stops in Melbourne. O'Brien had an unfortunate incident when one of his crew drowned. Slocum is remembered for displaying a dead shark and its progeny of 26 live young to the populace and thereby earning some money. He hired an Irishman to help with this enterprise but had to let him go 'owing to his over-stimulated enthusiasm'.

*Molly B* left Melbourne in the middle of the winter and sailed around Wilsons Prom and through Bass Strait. I stopped for a night in Refuge Cove, reputedly the most picturesque anchorage in Australia. It is well protected and preserved, being in the middle of a national park. It is popular in the summer but I had it all to myself. I rowed ashore and sat on a rock admiring the view. I turned around and there was a big wombat staring at me. It was about the size of a large pig. It lazily lumbered off into the bush.

Then I headed off up the east coast of Australia, stopping as I went in several small harbours. Most of these were quite sleepy, it being winter, and I came and went as I pleased. It was only at Gervis Bay that I got some attention. I accidently sailed through a target practice being run by the Royal Australian Navy. First they dive bombed me with their jets and then sent a launch out to tell me to get the hell out of the way. Then they sent a helicopter after me to take my photo. They seemed to have lots of hardware.

I sailed on to Sydney, passing famous Botany Bay and Bondi Beach. Little did I know that here in the beautiful harbour city I would meet someone who would change my life.

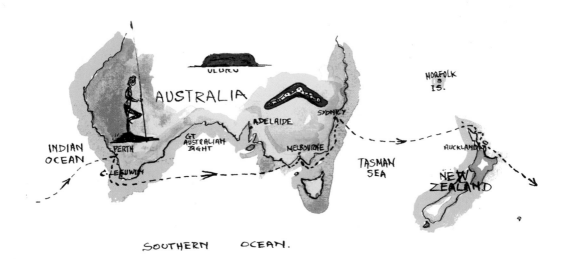

# Chapter 12

# 'Gracias a la Vida . . .'

*'Gracias a la vida que me ha dado tanto*
*Me dio dos luceros, que cuando los abro,*
*Perfecto distingo lo negro del blanco*
*Y en el alto cielo su fondo estrellado*
*Y en las multitudes el hombre que yo amo.'*

Lin and Larry Pardey, back in Freemantle, had told me to tie up at the Cruising Yacht Club in Sydney. I had written to Sydney asking them to keep letters for me. I added that I was the first Irish single hander to sail down to Australia. 'That should impress them,' I thought. They gave me a good welcome when I arrived. I became good friends there with the boatman 'The Bear' who had lost an arm to cancer. Bear was to go on to organise an entry in the Sydney Hobart race.

The Cruising Yacht Club no longer concerns itself much with cruising. It is now chiefly celebrated as the organiser of the famous Sydney to Hobart Yacht race. They discourage visiting yachts, not having the facilities or room. It is situated in the desirable location of Rushcutters Bay, prime yacht and residential real estate. The club kindly allowed *Molly B* to stay for the three months she was in Sydney. It shows how far the long distance voyaging craze has come in 30 years. When Francis Chichester sailed from England to Sydney in

1967 he was met by a huge welcoming flotilla. His boat, *Gipsy Moth 4*, was hauled out and he did any amount of alterations to it. The Queen knighted him. He was feted, wined and dined and he sailed on again hailed by another flotilla. Nowadays those who go a sailing have to pay their way.

There was a pile of letters for me at the yacht club, plus a small note on the notice board:

'For Peter Hogan. *Molly B* – Pl's phone Micaela.'

Australia is known as the lucky country. I called Micaela and she arrived down to Rushcutters Bay on Saturday morning to 'see the boat'. She was the friend of a friend of my sister Felicity. She had done some sailing, mostly in the Caribbean. 'I like to be on the water' is one of her bons mots. I don't think she was that impressed with the cabin of the 30 foot long *Molly B*. 'Where's the bed?' she asked, eyeing the forepeak full of buckets and sails. She was sitting on the bed. 'Ill show you later,' I winked.

We went for a sail out on the harbour and watched the start of a big ocean race. We did a tour of the local landmarks. That evening we went to her favourite Spanish restaurant – Capitan Torres – on Liverpool Street. Then we saw a flamenco performance. Then I walked her home.

*Molly B* was safely moored in Rushcutters Bay but I had run up on the rocks of true love. Micaela worked during the day as a Montessori teacher. An Irish mother and American dad had produced an exotic mix. A great linguist, she had many friends, particularly in the Mexican/Spanish community of Sydney. She had arrived in Australia five years earlier and liked the easy going sun-filled, laid back lifestyle. There was always something to do, a party, a concert, an exhibition or a BBQ. She introduced me to chorizo and tapas. We sat around on street side cafes watching the people go by. We shopped at the weekend markets. We went to the beach, to movies, swimming pools, galleries and restaurants. We took ferries round the harbour and buses out into the bush. *Molly B* lay forgotten in Rushcutters Bay.

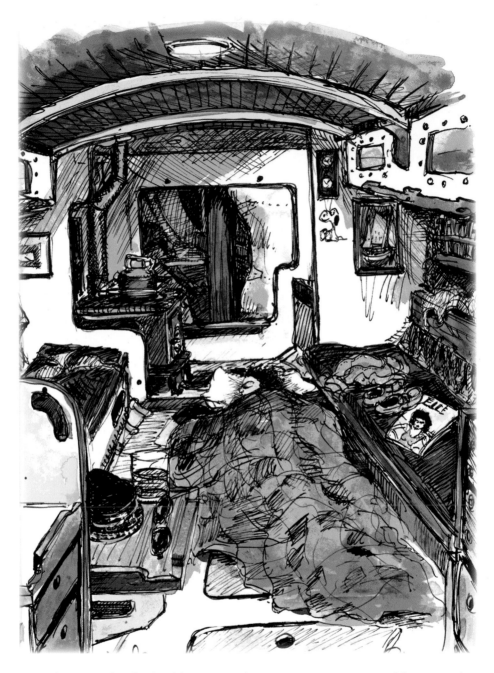

The months flashed by. Was the voyage going to end here on the rocks of true love? Micaela encouraged me to carry on. 'You are a man on a mission,' she said. 'You must finish that mission and then we will be together.'

So I decided to press on around the world. I returned to working on *Molly B* while Micaela was at school. I had a new storm jib made and extensive repairs to the mizzen and genoa. I checked over and replaced a lot of the rigging on the masts. I fitted a new inner 'baby' stay on the mainmast to give it more support. I dived on the barnacle-encrusted and fuzzy, moustachioed hull, scraping it clean. I stocked up again on food and spares.

Early in November I kissed Micaela goodbye as she went off to work. Tears flowed. I checked out of the Cruising Yacht Club and set sail bound for New Zealand, 1,000 miles away across the Tasman Sea.

It is early in the southern summer. I have a tough slow passage across the Tasman Sea, a stormy stretch of water. For the first six days *Molly B* is forced to the south away from my destination. There are headwinds, ferocious thunder, lightning, and rain showers. Then we make progress. I pass north around the tip of North Island inside the majestic three Kings Islands. New Zealand Coast Guard must have been keeping a keen eye out. They approached me in a launch and, perhaps observing *Molly B*'s erratic progress, asked me if 'I knew where I was?' I miss the chance to reply that I am looking for New Zealand. They direct me to Opua in the famous Bay of Islands.

Opua customs and excise quickly process me and admit me to the country. I had been anxious about any food I might have on board, having heard stories of the strict quarantine regime in New Zealand. The only thing they took was a cactus which had been on board since someone gave it to me in San Diego, 10 years previously. Off it went to the incinerator at the end of Opua town wharf.

The Bay of Islands is famous the world over as a Mecca for cruising boats. Here the great Eric Hiscock had ended his cruising days and where his last *Wanderer* had been built. Opua is the centre of activity as the port of entry. It is the natural end of the line for boats which have come across the Pacific by the trade wind route, from Panama or the west coast of the US. There is a thriving shipping business freighting cruising boats back to the United States from New Zealand.

Opua is very small. One shop, no pub and a small car ferry terminal. There is the Opua Cruising Club, a ramshackle shed which has the only pub in town. It runs weekly races and is very welcoming. Scattered about are several boatyards and most things which a boat might need are available or can be provided. It is very cruiser friendly. No one will tell you that you cannot hang your washing in the rigging or park your dinghy or overhaul your motor on the dock in Opua.

There is a 'net' operating each morning. At 8.00 am on channel 34 a volunteer yacht starts it up and it follows a set pattern: roll call, news, announcements, rides, trading information and any other business. For the first few days it is compelling listening. It allows me to get to know the district very quickly. After those initial first days it becomes a bit repetitive as the same information gets repeated for new arrivals. Where can one get a propane tank refilled and the times of the bus to Keri Keri? The big item on the net when I first arrive is the organisation of the forthcoming Thanksgiving dinner which is to be held in the Opua Cruising Club. One yacht has undertaken to arrange the cooking of 15 turkeys and is requesting boats to volunteer their ovens. *Molly B* cannot really help there, not having an oven.

There were many interesting cruising boats in the Bay of Islands. Two of these are of particular interest when I find them anchored in the sheltered coves of the Bay. The *Totorore* had made an amazing Antarctic circumnavigation which I had read about. The other was the converted Mediterranean work boat which the Austrian artist Hundertwasser had sailed out to New Zealand and where he now occasionally lived. I tried to find Hundertwasser's house, which was also famous for being built into a hill, out of recycled materials, but it is not open to the public. The artist himself is reported to be a great man for the ladies!

Micaela arrives for her Christmas break. I sail down to Auckland to meet her. We set off on a Christmas cruise almost immediately, meandering out through the islands of the Hauraki Gulf. We stop when we reach Great Barrier Island; a beautiful, forested, 40 mile long island which guards the entrance to the Hauraki Gulf. There is no need to go any further. Great Barrier is completely unspoilt and a nice mix of farming land and national park. We live on fresh oysters and champagne. We swim and sit in the sun. We walk through the forest. There is one restaurant on the island. When they see us coming they put Van Morrison on the sound system. We go to a Hangi

in a wool shed. A Hangi is the traditional Maori feast cooked on hot stones buried in a pit, dug in the ground. The team of men light the fire, heat the rocks, put them in a pit, wrap the food in leaves and cover the whole thing with soil. They then have a game of rugby, followed by a siesta. Then dinner is ready. Rock music and beer complete the tradition. Of all the islands I have visited on *Molly B*, Great Barrier is the one I would most like to revisit.

Micaela has to return to Sydney and her school. For me Cape Horn beckons. We sail back to Auckland where I prepare *Molly B* for her voyage around Cape Horn.

I dry *Molly B* out on the tide in Auckland and scrub and paint her. We are moored near the municipal market and this is a good place to stock up on basics like potatoes, onions, apples and oranges. The local kiwi fruit are very cheap as there is a worldwide glut. Auckland is a world class centre for boating, as everyone knows. Success in the Whitbread race and the America's Cup are as well known as are the

All Blacks rugby team. It is possible to get anything in the equip-ment line near where *Molly B* is docked. But my needs are simple. I buy a huge fisherman's smock in a chandlery and a big load of woolly jumpers from a charity shop for $1 apiece. That is my survival suit. I gather a big load of driftwood from the marina breakwater, fuel for the stove. I feel like the great early single hander Vito Dumas from Argentina who rounded Cape Horn in winter in a boat very similar to *Molly B*. He kept warm by stuffing newsprint down his oil skins!

Micaela finds a friend from Cork who owns the 'only Irish cafe in the southern hemisphere'. I think Finn wanted to own a pub but settled for a cafe. He is very helpful, driving me around and bringing me to supermarkets and such. Micaela spends her time teaching me how to bake bread and sprout alfalfa seeds in a plastic container.

It's getting late in the season as it will take me six weeks to cover the 5,000 miles to Cape Horn. It's do or die time. I give my trusty bike away and try to find a home for the dinghy. When no one wants it I decide to bring it along.

As I sail out of Auckland Micaela stands on the shore waving. She will fly back to Sydney.

# Chapter 13

# 'Because It's There'

*olly B* had a trouble free departure from Auckland and the Hauraki Gulf. Good offshore winds and flat seas propel the boat out into the middle of the Bay of Plenty and I make my departure from East Cape. This is the last land I will see for 5,000 miles. It's a bit like blasting off for the moon. Or jumping off a cliff.

I have a well practiced routine by this stage for preparing the boat at the start of a passage. All the various pieces of equipment which live on deck in port get stowed away. The anchor comes off the bow and ropes which are not being used are coiled and stowed. Fenders, buckets, boathooks, oars, cushions, fishing lines, towels and tools all find a place. Otherwise they would inevitably work themselves over the side. The cabin is a bit like a stall at a market. A crate of oranges, two bags of onions, two of potatoes, a box of tomatoes, a box of kiwi fruit and eight dozen eggs litter the main cabin. Other lesser quantities of fruit and vegetables also have to find a place where they will not roll about.

I start eating my way through the mountain of food which I do not expect to last – fresh bread, meat, cheese, carrots, greens, bananas.

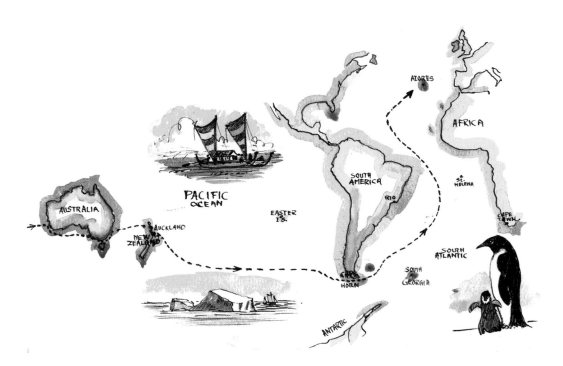

The plan from a navigation point of view was simple. Proceed south east to the 45th parallel and then 'run down my easting' on it until I approached the South American continent. Then dip down south and nip around the Horn which is on the 56th parallel of latitude. The distance is a bit longer than the great circle route which takes the intrepid sailor down south into the ice. Not for me.

There are no obstacles on the route – no islands, shoals or reefs. There is very little chance of meeting another ship. There are just the vast open reaches of the emptiest stormiest expanse of ocean in the world – the mighty Southern Ocean. This is why I have sailed this far. This is where Miles Smeeton was pitch poled, twice. This is where Al Hanson died. This is where Bernard Moitessier, Robin Knox Johnson and Rosie Swale made their names. This is Mount Everest.

Three days out from Auckland *Molly B* crosses the International Date Line. We gain a day. Magic really.

This extra day proves to be a humdinger of a sailing day also as *Molly B* clocks up a record noon to noon run. The clean underwater hull and the steady northwest wind, building up to a gale, pushes her on like an ocean racer. The hull, pushed to its limits, tries hopelessly to surf. But the motion is effortless and safe. We are not out of control as the self-steering vane works its magic. The occasional wave crashes across the deck. I drop the main sail and run all night under genoa and mizzen. I change down to jib at dawn then reef the mizzen. We surge on until midday as I count down the clock – a noon to noon run of 156 nautical miles.

*Molly B* screams on all that afternoon. I was hoping to repeat or better the performance and also worried that the wind might increase still further. But suddenly the wind died as the sun set and changed direction leaving a confused sea. *Molly B* stopped dead, sails slamming about in the lumpy sea. The following day at noon the distance run is down to 97 miles.

This watching the mileage and averages becomes a game driving me on. I drag out all the books on board and try to find reports of times taken by yachts on this route. O'Brien had a good run to the Horn, taking 40 days. His square sails come into their own on his heavy 50 footer, *Saoirse*. Chichester also, in his racing boat, makes good time. I had a private race with Alex Rose in *Lively Lady*. His boat is similar in size and displacement to *Molly B*. Knox Johnston made steady progress also in a similar type boat but was handicapped by a faulty self-steering system.

That first week of the passage, *Molly B* reels off 815 miles in the direction of Cape Horn. She was now in the roaring forties. There is no going back; it's a one way street. Even after one week, to sail back to New Zealand would necessitate a journey of perhaps 2,000 miles, first edging north across the westerlies and then working back in a big circle through the horse latitudes. In an emergency it would take less time and effort to make for a port in Chile. If a mast were to fall

down, if I broke a finger, if I got a tooth ache or should blow out all the sails, then Valparaiso is the logical destination for help.

I am soon repairing sails again. Kiwi contact cement does not match up to my favourite brand – Evo Stick. To put on a patch/

rubbing strip, first I stick with contact glue and then laboriously sew around the edges to stop the patch flapping itself off. I was using up a lot of sail makers needles. They break easily. You push the needle through the layers of tough sailcloth with a metal thimble then pull it clear with a pliers. That's one stitch.

The furious pace continued throughout the second week. *Molly B* clocked up an impressive 840 miles for the seven days. It was getting chilly and quite an effort to take a bath up on the foredeck. At times it was misty and foggy and I thought we must be touching the waters of the Antarctic Ocean. But the water stayed the beautiful deep blue azure of the South Pacific.

I was now well into shipboard routine, a world of my own. My appetite returned and I was eating my way through the ripening vegetables and fruit. The kiwi were lasting very well, the tomatoes nearly gone. I note in the log that I have only opened three tins so far. I catch a tuna. I also see a big whale, perhaps a blue whale. It slides alongside, almost part of the waves, snorts into the air and is gone. This was to be the only big, full-sized whale I saw in the southern ocean.

Morale was high as the miles gurgle past astern. The pattern of the wind systems passing through repeats itself. The wind builds up from the south, passes around through west and then blows itself out as it passes through north taking about three or four days to complete the cycle. Then it leaves a confused sea in which *Molly B* flops about waiting for a new wind. Sometimes there was nothing I could do except drop the sails. But I never had to wait very long for a new wind. It builds steadily from the south, the waves gradually succumb to its authority and *Molly B* falls into step again. Off we go.

We were half way to the Horn. The sails and the rig continue to need much attention. The gaff jaws, the Achilles heel of the gaff rig, were the neediest. Hiscock was adamant that the gaff rig was not suitable for voyaging, and he was my hero. He was right. But I am accustomed to problems with the gaff jaws by now and resigned to the fact that they will have to be repaired every few thousand miles or so. It's a bit like servicing a car.

By the fourth week out *Molly B* was still hugging the 45 degree parallel of latitude and about 1,200 miles from the coast of Chile. It was time to start thinking of easing further down to the south. Cape Horn is at 56 degrees south. This is an unromantic way of expressing how a great journey is made. It reduces the problem to crossing a piece of graph paper rather than the greatest ocean in the world.

Then I saw a ship on the horizon. A boxy shape with a superstructure amidships rolling along in the big swells. I switched on the VHF and I was soon talking to Ross Finlay on the bridge of the *Australian Venture*. She was out of Melbourne and bound around Cape Horn to Europe. We discussed the weather, where we were going and even dipped into sport. She was following the 45 degree line just as *Molly B* was and keeping above the line of ice on the pilot chart. Ross said that there was much ice this year but that it was all well to the south. I asked him to drop a line to my Dad and he promised to

do so when the ship docked in England. (He did.) I asked him why his ship did not use the Panama Canal. He said that it was expensive to transit the canal and did not save much time. His company had a sailing to Europe each week around the Horn. After a certain amount of searching he found *Molly B* as a small blip on his radar. As *Australian Venture* disappeared over the horizon it was comforting to know that somebody, somewhere, knew that I had got this far.

*Molly B* turned to the south heading for Cape Horn at the end of week five. Soon we are crossing the 50 degree south latitude line. In the southern ocean this is known as the screaming fifties. Now *Molly B* is on the small-scale chart which I have of the tip of South America. The waves build up with the wind and now and then break across the deck. The most common rig combination now is the reefed mizzen and storm jib. Every now and then the waves will catch the thin plywood vane of the self-steerer and snap it off where it is attached to the stainless holder. I have a replacement ready and cleverly make a smaller version for use in heavy weather. Big southern ocean rollers occasionally result in a complete knockdown as *Molly B* spews around broadside and gets caught in the breaking crest of a wave. The first time this happens a lot of water comes spouting in through the companionway hatch and on to the chart table. I fear that the radio and GPS could be immersed in water. I solve this little problem by covering them in plastic!

I rarely now spend much time on deck. I rush out to change the rig or sails, adjust the ropes, check for chafe or something working itself loose. When I do this I wrap up well in two of everything. Two sets of pants, two oilskins, two safety harnesses, a damp towel around my neck, a woolly hat and rubber boots. I clamber up on deck into the slipstream, make sure I am well hooked on, close the hatch behind me and do what I have to do. I winch in a few inches of jib, tighten down on the kicker of the mizzen, adjust the self-steerer slightly, stow an errant trailing line. I do a quick check on the foredeck and rigging and dash below again before a wave breaks. The boat is like a sealed bottle or maybe even a submarine.

We are approaching the west coast of Chile as we head south for Cape Horn. But I do not want to get too close to this potential lee shore before we reach the correct southern latitude. *Molly B* is slightly out of control as she makes her approach. I have to tack downwind as I position *Molly B* to go around Cape Horn. Jibing is not easy in the high winds. As the boat turns dead downwind the storm jib slams from side to side with incredible force. It's a bit like a giant whiplash which puts a great strain on the sail, the mast and the forestay. I am sure one of them will go. At the same time I am steering, having disconnected the self-steerer and have to jibe the mizzen. This involves releasing the vang, pulling in on its boom so it will not hit the self-steerer. Then I pull in on its topping lift to raise the boom. Next pulling in on the sheet I cause it to jibe. The boat spews around on a wave and takes up its new course. I reconnect the self-steerer and the vang. I then bring the jib across and adjust the sheets. We are off on a new tack downwind. The waves break all round striking *Molly B* on the stern quarter.

I get it wrong once and jibe against the boom vang. BANG. The mizzen boom breaks in two as it pulls against its preventer. Almost a day's work goes into splicing the boom back together with some spare wood and nuts and bolts.

The water is everywhere, finding holes and dribbles in the fibre-glass which I never imagined existed. They drip down on me as I lie on the bunk. Everything is damp. The boat crashes onward, the waves rolling right over it. I take the spray dodgers off to give the waves an unobstructed passage across the decks. It is very tiring to do anything other than lie on the bunk. I rarely bother to look out at the horizon. The ice is supposed to be to the south. *Molly B* tacks downwind in a broad fairway on the pilot chart between the land and the ice line on the chart. Eating is the high point of the day. That lasts for about five minutes. I cook up a big mess of rice, potatoes or spaghetti once every two days. The leftovers last for the following day. I wolf the food down straight out of the pan, burning my mouth in the process and collapse on the bunk to sleep it off. *Molly B* crashes onwards to the south.

At the end of the sixth week *Molly B* had run a distance of 881 miles for the week and most of that under storm jib alone. This was the best week's run I was ever to do on *Molly B*. But record week's runs were not really on my mind at that stage. Cape Horn was 329 miles away to the south east. In three days I could expect to round Cape Horn.

This was how it transpired. The barometer was dropping. The sea turned an icier colour and the number and types of birds increased. The islands of southern Chile were near. In the afternoon a hazy sun came out with a 'mackerel' sky, indications of approaching bad weather.

The wind built up over the afternoon. I reduced sail. First the mainsail came down, and then the jib got replaced by the storm jib. Around midnight as *Molly B* screamed along I dropped the reefed mizzen leaving the tiny storm jib to react with the self-steerer as

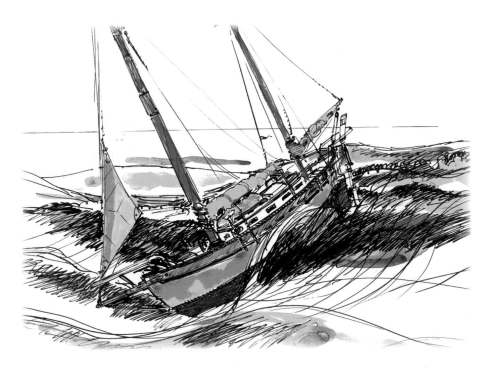

we crashed along. The strain on the forestay was extreme. I could not reduce sail any further. It was a sleepless night. In the morning a breaking wave carried away the plywood vane. I replaced it with the smallest vane I had. I had a big breakfast, like a gladiator getting ready for battle. A tin of apricots, ham and eggs, fried bread (an Irish delicacy) coffee and biscuits with peanut butter and marmalade. At noon I was 220 miles away from the Horn. The barometer was still dropping and the sea building up. I ran on under storm jib making a steady 6.5 knots with the tiny sail. Occasionally the hull would attempt to surf and the waves run clear over the cabin. I catnapped in my oilskins putting on a second set when going on deck. It was an anxious time. How much worse could it get was the question I kept asking myself. *Molly B* was now pretty much out of control as she ran downwind. The jib at times would crack from side to side putting a huge strain on the forestay and mast. The whole boat shook when it did this. The self-steerer worked overtime, often completely underwater except for its faithful vane. By adjusting the self-steerer to bring *Molly B* more across the wind I could stop the jib from flapping back and forth.

Cape Horn was now 95 miles away. Diego Ramirez Island, a small outlying reef, was some 60 miles distant and *Molly B* was about to pass over an underwater shelf where the depth changes from the 2,000 meters of the south Pacific up to the shallow reef running out from the tip of South America. This is one of the main reasons Cape Horn is so dangerous. I planned to pass in between Diego Ramirez and the Horn. The barometer was still dropping. The storm was now probably at its peak.

At times we recorded speeds of up to eight knots just with the storm jib. There was a strong current sluicing through between Cape Horn and Antarctica. I stood in the companionway looking at the overworked self steerer. I skipped between the chart, the GPS and the barometer. The jib whipped back and forth and the waves broke over the cabin. 'Something's got to give,' I thought. There was little I could do. I felt like a man locked in a barrel heading down river to roll over Niagara Falls.

By late afternoon *Molly B* was very near to Diego Ramirez Island but I never saw it in the fading light. I had other things on my mind. Twice *Molly B* was knocked down by breaking waves, the mast at least horizontal with the water. Perhaps it was the disturbed sea caused by the underwater shelf. I was kept busy replacing the vane on the self-steerer. With less than 60 miles to go to the Horn I began to feel more confident. 'It's in the bag,' I thought.

I did some calculations. It looked as though *Molly B* was going to sail past Cape Horn in the night. 'It would be nice to see it,' I thought. Having come all this way. I decided to try and heave to by using the mizzen sail to hold the bow into the wind. I dropped the jib. I hauled up the flapping reefed mizzen hoping that it would hold the bow into the wind. But in the space of about five minutes it simply flapped itself to pieces. I decided to try laying ahull with no sails up. I lashed the tiller, secured everything on deck and went below. I

was standing around in the cabin, getting the feel of the boat under this new, sail-less, condition and preparing to take off my oilskins. It was dark in the cabin and I was holding a flashlight in my hand.

Suddenly and without warning and with an almighty WHOOSH followed by a huge BANG, with the impact of an express train, a wave hit the side of *Molly B*. Over she went and I found myself calmly walking up along the bookcases on the port side of the cabin. Everything went quiet as *Molly B* reached the top of her roll. There was a moment of stillness as I looked about with the flashlight in my hand. At the companionway I could see the water spurting in through the hatch like it used to do on sinking submarines in movies on TV. Forward I noted that the mast was at an odd angle. Then I realized the boat was upside down. Then slowly, like a heavy, steady pendulum the hull righted itself.

*Molly B* had turned turtle but had come back up on the side she went over. It was not a 360 capsize. There was a terrible mess down below but I immediately went topsides to check everything. The masts were still standing. My first thought was to get us sailing again. There was no reason why another wave should not come along, hit us sideways and turn the boat over again. And this time with me on deck. Then I notice that the main stay of the mast had sheared somehow. I tried securing it but could not unravel the twisted rigging in the dark. I then discovered that the sacrificial safety tube of the self-steering paddle had sheared. The boat must have lurched violently to the side. It's a big job to replace the paddle. So no self-steering. I grabbed the tiller and started steering through the spin drift, running down wind under bare poles and taking the waves on the quarter.

I steered all night, crossing the reef between Cape Horn and Diego Ramirez. A full moon came up. It was very beautiful, the silver sky turning the clouds, waves, boat and myself into the same ghost white like silhouette. There did not seem to be much danger as long as I kept steering and pointing the stern of *Molly B* into the oncoming rollers. It got cold. I piled on the sweaters and woolly hats. I ran a line from the tiller through blocks so I could steer from the shelter of the companionway. I got tired. I shook my head and stamped my feet and kept steering.

By early the next morning it seemed that the seas had become more regular and less threatening. There was not much sign of the wind abating. Perhaps in the northwest wind we were getting some shelter from the land. I lay down and had a catnap.

When I awoke things seemed a lot better. I found a shackle and some tools. I unravelled the rigging and got the mainmast stay set up again. I replaced the tube on the self-steerer. This was no easy task as it involved climbing out over the stern to get at the vane mechanism. I hoisted the storm jib. Then with the dawn fully over I looked up to the north and saw in the distance the faint grey shape of the most famous and most feared headland in the world, Cape Horn.

I was exhausted. I slept a bit more then got up. Cape Horn was still there. The sea was in a confused lumpy state. I tried motoring towards Cape Horn to get a better look. There was a strong current

pushing *Molly B* to the east and I made little progress in the lumpy sea. I slept some more, did further repairs, slept, repaired and so on. To do even the simplest thing was exhausting. The mizzen boom had again been broken. The mainsail, furled on its boom, had burst beyond repair by the force of the knockdown. I bent on the spare.

The wind continued to ease off and gave two days of respite in which to recover. I thought of heading for the Falkland Islands to regroup and repair. Then I decided to keep going.

I lit the stove. I put some of Micaela's music on the ghetto blaster – Yothu Yindi, an aboriginal rock group. I looked around at the confusion of the cabin, this thing I had built. Tools all over the place, books, charts, blankets, clothes, food, bits of string. My whole idiotic world. Cape Horn was on the distant horizon. And I broke down and I cried, a sort of a happy cry.

# Chapter 14

# 'Home is the Sailor'

*'Home is the sailor*
*Home from the sea.'*

There was a ferocious current pushing *Molly B* to the east. I got the sails working and soon Cape Horn was out of sight well to the northwest. A westerly wind blew up as we headed north. I pinched up into the wind in an attempt to pass close to the Falklands Islands, 300 miles to the north. When I arrived off Port Stanley it was a good 35 miles to the west and directly upwind. I could not see the land in the thick, misty conditions. I could hear the local radio station playing English pop music. I tried calling on VHF but got no reply. I pressed on to the north.

It had taken *Molly B* 45 days to sail the 5,000 miles from Auckland to the Horn. I now had a further 7,000 miles to go before reaching my planned next stop which was the Azores Islands far off the coast of Portugal. This turned out to be a bit of a marathon.

To sail from Cape Horn to the Azores is a complex zig zag course spanning seven different wind systems. I will name them. First there are the westerlies of the southern ocean which pushed *Molly B* out into the middle of the south Atlantic. Next are the horse latitudes – calms and variables. Then there are the south east trade

winds blowing up to the equator. The doldrums hang around about the equator. Then come the band of north east trade winds across which the sailboat has to beat. Then there are the variables of the northern hemisphere, mainly calms. Finally the westerlies of the north Atlantic waft the weary traveller back home.

*Molly B* set out on this epic slog. I made good progress in the westerlies heading north out of the southern ocean, the roaring forties, rogue waves, albatrosses and all that stuff. As a parting gift from the southern ocean I caught another tuna to keep me going. Food, while not a problem, was getting pretty basic. The three staples of rice, pasta and potatoes were rotated monotonously. But I am not complaining. Hunger is a strange thing, difficult to describe. A bit like a thirst. A hungry man can eat with relish rice fried in cooking oil and enjoy it as much as a meal in a fancy restaurant. The body becomes a sponge which soaks up the nourishment. I took vitamins and had fresh oranges and lemons all the way. I used Micaela's trick with a plastic container to sprout seeds. It took about a week to produce one salad! Francis Chichester had also been a fan of sprouting. Silly food such as popcorn or packet cake mixes were valuable in tricking the body into thinking it was full. It's a good job I was alone though. I think I might have had a mutiny on my hands if there had been a crew.

Joshua Slocum's writing about food is amusing. He was famous for his doughnuts, fried in batter, and also for a batch of plums which gave him nightmares. Bernard Moitessier was more French in his tastes, living on seabirds and free samples from the food companies. Conor O'Brien does not much mention food. It was probably cooked by his paid hands on his solid fuel stove.

Now fish became an important addition to the larder. The fishing gear is simple yet effective. Sea fishing is an unsubtle affair, unlike its river counterpart. The hook is large and strong, as shiny as possible. It can be wrapped in a shiny piece of tin or scrap material. Next comes a strong length of wire or heavy gut as a trace, maybe about three metres long. This can be attached to a swivel if one is available. Then comes maybe a weight of some sort, though this is not essential, and should be of a shape which will not spin in the wake. Next comes the actual fishing line, strong thick nylon about at least 100 metres. This has to be attached to a length of shock cord which is tied to the boat. Also essential is a sturdy gaff for getting the catch on board.

I was always impressed by Francis Chichester who often stated in his books that he did not fish because it slowed down the boat. A true racing man. I was not that concerned with the drag of the fishing line slowing *Molly B* as long as there seemed some prospect of a catch. But a catch was not that common an event. I only fished when I was in attendance on the line and success seemed likely. I did not tow the line endlessly day and night.

It is exciting when a fish strikes. The shock cord goes taught and the line veers from side to side. I pull in the heavy line using a pair of gloves. It is always a big fish. A tuna in the cold high latitudes or a dorado in the tropics. As it nears the boat it trashes from side to side and jumps clear of the water in attempts to throw the hook. It is still fresh and full of fight. I let the line back out and the shock cord does its work. I make a cup of tea. The boat sails on dragging the struggling fish. Half an hour, an hour later, the fish tires. It gives up the struggle against the constant drag. It goes limp and rises to the top of the water. It surfs along on the waves seemingly dead. Again I pull in the line slowly, gaff at the ready. As the fish nears the dark hull it shoots off again, fighting and jumping. Maybe I will give it a few more miles being dragged along. Again I haul in the line. Slowly and

smoothly it comes alongside amidships. I get the gaff under its thick belly. In a sharp upward jerk I do the business. The fish comes alive thrashing and flailing about. Over the lifelines and on to the deck with it. Blood everywhere as it struggles on the side deck. The line tangles up in everything. Wearing sea boots is a good idea. Out with the biggest knife on board and that's it. Four big fillets of prime tuna in a bucket, the rest goes overboard to the sharks. I store the catch in the bilge. Fish for dinner for the next four days.

As we headed north into the horse latitudes I crossed the Rio de la Plata to Cape Town shipping lane. I espied a ship and they sent a fax off for me to my Dad who was much relieved to hear that I had rounded the Horn. He rushed off to tell his buddies in the yacht club.

I studied the charts constantly. I was tempted to pull into a port in South America. Rio de La Plata or Rio de Janero.

I spent much time sitting in the cockpit sticking and sowing patches on to the sails. The mizzen especially, the most frequently used sail on board, was in bad shape. The main also required constant attention.

As *Molly B* approached the tropics I devised a new way to collect rainwater. Previously I had simply filled buckets from rain running off the sails and in very heavy downpours was able to decant some of this into the tanks. Now I refined this system by adding a sort of gutter and drain pipe to the mizzen boom. This ran to a jerry can in the cockpit. Now I had as much fresh water as I could use. I was even able to do some laundry.

I managed to keep up an average of about 100 miles a day for the passage to the Azores but it was hard work. My hat goes off to those clipper captains of yore who brought big, heavy, square-rigged ships along this route. They are reputed to have been able to average 200 miles a day as they brought the tea and wool to London.

I spent a memorable night becalmed on the equator. It was a clear, star-studded night. I sat in the cockpit watching the stars and wondering when they would change from the southern hemisphere to the north. I turned on the VHF and heard the guttural voices of some fishermen talking in Portuguese. I was afraid to announce my presence. They might be pirates.

I had better luck with the doldrums this time, not being worried that we would be pushed off course. It helped also that I was going home. Morale was high and I knew better how to control *Molly B* in difficult conditions, when to push her and when to drop the sails and simply wait.

The journey though was too long for the slow *Molly B*. It was too long a period of time to spend alone even for a reclusive sort like myself. Sailors now have broken the speed and the communication barriers. Anyone can whiz around the world in 80 days or less and be online every inch of the way talking and sending pictures. I lay on the bunk and listened to John Peel on the world service of the BBC or Garrison Keillor on the Voice of America and waited for a favourable wind.

*Molly B* entered the north east trade winds and headed up to windward. The warm blue spray whipped across the deck. The salt coated everything. The sheets strained in their blocks and the hull took up a steady hobby horse motion as it surged across the waves at an angle. We were heading for Florida. I crossed the New York to the Cape shipping route. The water was full of floating waste. Big tankers and bulk carriers from the industrial east coast of the United States bringing raw material to feed the furnaces. I sailed on. Then *Molly B* could turn to the east again and head for the Azores.

*Molly B* docked in Horta, on the island of Faial in the Azores, 117 days after leaving Auckland, New Zealand. Horta is a yachting Mecca, a cross roads in the middle of the Atlantic, important as such since the dawn of discovery. The yachts are a recent arrival. They are made very welcome in the new marina and a local industry has grown up to service them.

The paintings are famous. All around, on every wall and pavement yachts and boats have left their name and date. Many leave a colourful picture, verse or crew list and destination. It is a tradition as long as voyaging – to leave a token, a record. In many places in the world if you painted a picture on the marina wall you would be arrested. In Horta it has become an art form.

Dad, back in Dublin, still recovering from cancer, jumped on a plane. Accompanied by my brother-in-law Pat, they flew down to Lisbon and then out to meet and greet me. Probably cost more than the entire trip had cost me with *Molly B*, but it was a nice gesture. They brought an immense fruitcake with them. Each evening they wined and dined me in the beautiful parador nearby. We went and looked at the still active volcano on Faial.

Pat and I hung out in the famous Peter's Café Sport. The original Peter had been friendly to the early voyagers who stopped in Horta and it is mentioned in countless voyaging books as a welcoming place. Now it is a bit of a disco, run by the family of the original Peter. There is a small museum section upstairs dedicated to whaling, scrimshaw and to the early voyagers who frequented the place.

Dad and Pat departed for Lisbon and home. I departed the following day in the company of an American in a Tahiti ketch who I had befriended. He was also sailing round the world. He was using an electric auto pilot and was having endless trouble with it. Or rather them, as he kept having to replace them as they burnt out. I told him to get a wind vane.

The passage in to the Irish coast was speedy and efficient. I dropped anchor in Baltimore harbour eight days after leaving Horta. No one took much notice of the beat up little ketch anchored in the harbour. They are used to more exotic fare in Baltimore. This is where Conor O'Brien had his boats built, along the lines of the local workboats. I made some phone calls from the pub and my brother Neil rushed down from Cork city to greet me. I bought some bacon and eggs in the local shops and sailed on up to Dublin.

In Dublin there was a nice welcoming reception, mainly from the buddies of my Dad. They had been getting a blow by blow account of my progress over the last 18 months whether they liked it or not. They made me an honorary member of the club.

Micaela jumped on a plane and in short order was congratulating me too. To say we had a great reunion would be an understatement. I put *Molly B* on a mooring and forgot about her for the rest of the summer.

In autumn *Molly B* returned to her usual winter mooring in the Liffey river. I lifted her out of the water and that was that for a while. Micaela had taken her place in my affections.

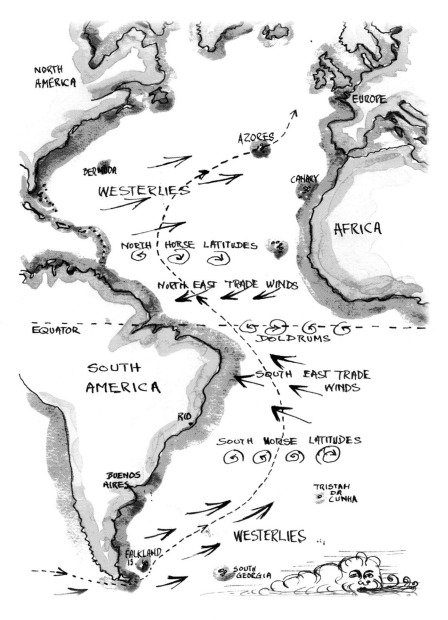

# Chapter 15

# 'On a Slow Boat to China'

*'I'd like to get you*
*On a slow boat to China,*
*All to myself alone.'*

**M**olly B spent the winter in the Grand Canal Dock area of Dublin. Neglected and forgotten. I was giving my undivided attention to Micaela. That, and attempting to get on with my working life. It was a long distance love affair. Micaela returned to Sydney, I flew out and stayed with her. The following year she arrived in Dublin with her boxes on a one way ticket. We were inseparable.

One day I said, 'Let's sail away to China. We have a boat and we might as well use it.' So began the 'Slow Boat to China Voyage'. I think it was the auld ones in Ringsend who gave us the idea, certainly the name. Every time we went into a bar they would start singing the old hit, 'I'd like to get you on a slow boat to China all for my very own', dancing around the place. Maybe considering what subsequently happened the song is worth quoting in full:

*I'd like to get you*
*On a slow boat to China,*
*All to myself alone.*
*To get you and keep you in my arms evermore,*
*Leave all your lovers*
*Weeping on the faraway shore.*
*Out on the briny*
*With the moon big and shinny,*
*Melting your heart of stone.*
*Darling, I'd love to get you*
*On a slow boat to China,*
*All to myself alone.*

I thought I would like to visit Kamchatka and that's reasonably near China. I had never heard of any boat sailing that way. Micaela was a great traveller in a previous existence. My days as a reclusive single hander were over.

We got a considerable amount of sponsorship and publicity when we announced that we were going to embark on this venture. Among many other things Watson Sails donated a set of sails. A businessman gave us new rigging, Irish Distillers threw in a lot of anchoring equipment and friends rallied round helping in all sorts of ways. *Molly B* was spruced up like she had never been before.

The plan was to sail over to France, go through the Canal du Midi and sail across the Mediterranean. Then we would transit the Suez Canal, sail through the Red Sea, across the Indian Ocean, through the straits of Malacca and on up to China. I had in the back of my mind that I would end the voyage in Vancouver, a sort of fitting homecoming for *Molly B*. It did not really work out like that.

We organised a big bash for a send-off. My old school chum Dick Spring was running the country at the time. He agreed to come along and send us off from the river Liffey.

It was the biggest party I have ever organised. Dick turned up with his fleet of state cars and gave a nice speech which was reported by all the newspapers. *Molly B* was weighted down to the gunnels by

the mass of presents and offerings which people presented to us. It
was a nice sunny morning as we steamed down the Liffey, a small
flotilla of well wishers alongside. *Molly B* pulled into Wicklow to take
a breather and do some stowing. The November weather stayed fine
as we pushed on down the coast to Dunmore East where it changed.
November gales descended and we sat in the harbour and considered
our options.

While *Molly B* might have had
new sails, rigging and anchors she
was the same basic 30 foot double
ender which I had sailed around the
world in on my own. Now there
were the two of us on board. The
loo was a bucket in the forepeak.
The shower was that same bucket
up on the foredeck. There was a two

burner Primus stove, when both burners were working. There was
no electricity or anything fancy like that and only a limited supply
(80 gallons) of fresh water. It was the start of the autumn equinox
season when bad weather can be expected. We were proposing to sail
across the English Channel and then into the Bay of Biscay in these
conditions. Micaela looked me in the eye and asked me did I think it
was safe. I replied that a prudent yachtsman probably would not do
what we were about to do. So we decided that Micaela would travel
overland and meet me in Bordeaux.

Micaela headed off to strike-bound France where she had a great
time with her friends in Paris. I waited in Dunmore East on the
*Molly B* watching for a weather window to head south. After a few
days I set out and thrashed across the Bristol Channel. I dropped
anchor in the Scilly Isles, there to wait some more. I got fed up waiting and so retreated to the little port of Penzance at the tip of Cornwall. There I ran into my old buddies of five years earlier, Lin and
Larry Pardey, who were wintering in nearby Falmouth. We spent a

wonderful evening together and they showed me where they were overhauling Talesin on their endless cruise. That was the last time I was to see them.

*Molly B* waited in Penzance for a few days. Then in a daring night sail she crossed the English Channel close hauled and managed, just, to ease around the tip of Brittany and into the Bay of Biscay.

Things improved after that. The winds eased up, the sun came out, we had made our escape. *Molly B* was heading for the estuary of the Gironde river, 120 miles to the south. I dropped anchor for the night at Royanne with its modern, striking church. All about are the remains of military fortifications. The Gironde estuary was important strategically and very heavily fought over during the war. There are still huge submarine bases in the river, large concrete constructions now used for yachts and fishing boats.

The estuary is a wonderful inland sea, wending its way into the heart of prime French wine country. The beautifully tended vineyards slope gently down to the sea. Dotted about in their midst were magnificent chateau. From the entrance on the Bay of Biscay to Bordeaux is about 70 miles. *Molly B* did it with sails and motor in two wonderful days of inland sailing. The life of the estuary, the shipping, the fishermen, the villages, the trees, the birds making it a memorable jaunt.

I got to a phone and called Micaela in Paris. She had been worried. France was on general strike. They take industrial action seriously in France. Nothing was moving. We arranged to meet in Bordeaux.

Bordeaux is a beautiful town. Apart from its association with wine it has many attractions in its historic old quarter. I tied *Molly B* up to some old barges on the river below one of the magnificent bridges over the Gironde. I turned on the VHF in the morning. A French chap was asking if 'the yacht *Molly B* could receive me'. Indeed I could. Shortly I was talking to Micaela. And so we were reunited.

We returned to the historic town of Pauillac to have the masts of *Molly B* lifted. Here there is a neat little harbour on the river with a crane which they use for stepping masts. I was able to neatly stow the masts with one end on the hefty gallows spanning the cabin and the other ends on the bow. The relatively short length of the mast on a gaff rigged boat is here an advantage. Pauillac is a famous wine centre and there is a wine shop there to beat the band. It is dangerous to ask advice about wines in this shop. They are accustomed to big spenders.

*Molly B* proceeded happily up the Gironde past Bordeaux. We were now above the tidal reaches of the Gironde. The river, particularly in winter, flows fast and strong. It was all that *Molly B*'s motor could do to push us up stream to the connection with the start of the canal system. This is at a place called Castets.

The crossing of France to the Mediterranean involves the use of two canals. The Canal Lateral au Gironde as far as Toulouse and then the Canal du Midi to complete the connection to the Med. Combined, the two canals are called the Canal des Deux Mers. It is a famous and recognised route, sections of it dating back to 1680s. An engineering marvel, it no longer has commercial traffic but has a lot of tourist activity in the summer. To transit in winter, as we were going to do, was unusual and exciting.

It was Christmas. France was on general strike. The canal workers were on holiday. Here we had to stay in Castets till the holiday was over and the keepers of the canal could give us our papers and allow *Molly B* to lock up onto the canal.

But we were together doing what we wanted to do. It was our big adventure. The French seemed to understand. Always there were smiles and handshakes. Waves from the workmen and toilers in the fields. I think we must have looked like something out of a Babar book. One could tell from looking at *Molly B* and her crew that they were going far. This was not one of the normal class of vessel transiting the canal. This was more Jules Verne brought up to date.

Micaela studied the local cuisine, coming from a family of gourmets. She sought out whatever local dish or cassoulet was associated with the region and we tried it. Thus we had a memorable Christmas dinner tied to the wharf below the huge lock at Castets.

We waited out the holiday without much bother. A local musician entertained us for a day in his restored farmhouse. We took the

bus back to Bordeaux. The frost covered the deck and the landscape each night but the stove down in the cabin kept the interior nice and snug. I roamed the canal banks with my bushman's saw cutting firewood.

Then we got under way. The canal employees are a great bunch. Dependable and hard working, but they move at their own pace. 'They grind slow, but they grind exceeding fine.' They send us on our way. The first 53 locks of the Canal du Garonne cover the 150 miles to Toulouse. The canal winds its way through beautiful pastoral country-side. It follows and feeds off the wild Garonne which used to be the waterway. It is not wine country but much of it is famous for its prunes and other fruit. The neat rows of fruit trees were endless. It was the pruning season. The workers in their heavy green jackets clipped away at the redundant branches turning the trees into almost

identical sculptures. But each one was different. In the middle of the fields are the wonderful classical round pigeonniers.

The villages skirting the canal are silent and timeless. There were few people about. They have all gone to the cities. We would usually moor near a small village, have our evening meal and then walk into the town to do a small shop and view the church. It could have been 1930. It could have been 1830. We slept on the floor of *Molly B*. It is the only space big enough to make a double bed with the two cushions from the seat berths. It's a small but comfortable cabin for two people, the sleeping bags piled on top and the wood stove smouldering away.

Agen is the first big town along the route. Here there is a fine aqueduct bringing the canal over the Gironde. Here I could get diesel as the boat marinas dotted along the way were all closed. I had to lug two jerry cans to a car filling station.

Next was Moissac, another historical town with its famous abbey, cloisters and tympanum. Here we had to stop. The canal was closed. They were cleaning and were not expecting winter traffic. We pleaded with the canal workers. Let us go through. They let us stew for a few days and then a manager came and instructed the lock keeper to let us proceed. Off we went. The level of the water in the section was low and they did not expect us to get through. There was a danger we might get stuck. They kindly allowed the section to fill up for us.

We were approaching Toulouse. I was expecting an industrial town but in fact the centre of Toulouse is lovely, as nice as Bordeaux. We stayed here for a night in the centre of town. I got up in the middle of the night hearing a footfall on the deck. A vagabond or someone was up to no good. I popped my head out of the cabin and he scurried away into the cold night. He did not expect to find someone on board in the middle of January.

Next was the actual Canal du Midi which would take us to the Med. The locks and settings are beautiful and ancient. Cut stone locks of oval shape and mature trees winding through the Mediter-

annian landscape. The canal has had 400 years to blend itself into the locale. If the Three Musketeers had ridden up the towpath I would not have been surprised.

*Molly B* crossed over the watershed and started descending towards the Med. The landscape became more quaint rustic, less industrial farming. We arrived at Carcassonne with its restored fortress and spent a day doing the tourist rounds. Then it was on across the swampy region of the Aude to the wonderful five-step set of locks at Beziers.

It started to rain a lot but *Molly B* had the bit between her teeth. We could smell the sea. We passed through the confusing three-way lock at Agde and out onto the Etang du Thau. Salt water. We motored on through acres of oyster farms. In the distance I saw something pink. I called to Micaela as we putted through a huge flock of flamingoes. The nice man in the bridge control at Sete let us use the showers near his office.

We had arrived at the end of the canal. The Mediterranean awaited.

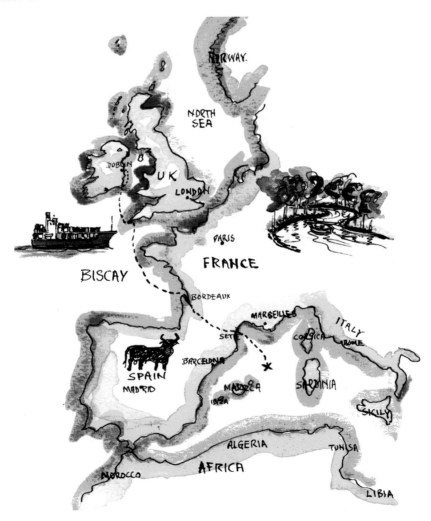

# Chapter 16

# 'I'll Never Get Out of This World Alive'

*'Now you're lookin' at a man that's gettin' kinda mad*
*I had lots of luck but it's all been bad*
*No matter how I struggle and strive*
*I'll never get out of this world alive.'*

It was mid-March, still very early in the season to go sailing on the Med. It took us a few days to get settled in Sete. It is a big fishing town nestled around a large hill – Mont St Clair – on the swampy shores of the Med. We found a man who would lift *Molly B*'s masts back in. Then we found a berth in the outer harbour in a marina where we waited for better weather. And we waited and we waited and we waited. The rain poured down and the wind whistled and roared in the rigging. I doubled up the dock lines. The masts of the boats around rattled and banged and whined. The surge from the waves battering the sea wall nearby pushed everything around violently. The Med was in an ugly mood. I had not realised that it could be such a tempestuous sea in winter. Virtually all yacht traffic ceases.

We amused ourselves as best we could around and about Sete and the seafront. We got friendly with an English bloke who had a big motor launch and was very familiar with the European canals. He helped me with *Molly B*'s motor. We visited weekend markets. We searched for good value restaurants.

Micaela is never happier than when munching away on sea food. In the restaurants and fish shops of Sete she was in her element. She also enjoyed being in an exotic milieu, street markets, foreign languages, colourful characters. But cooped up on board *Molly B* there were problems. A lot of these centred on the lack of much, or any, washing facilities on board *Molly B*. To make a long story short we had a row, or disagreement, or something. I asked Micaela to get off the boat. I walked her to the train station and she got on a train for Paris. And that was that. In retrospect, it was probably the luckiest day of her life.

'I go on,' I said. 'The voyage goes on. To Hell with her.' *She has given up her life in Australia to be with you.* 'Well, I'm worth it.' *She loves you.* 'So what.' *If she wants to wash her hair every morning she cannot be serious about sailing to China.* 'Women!' *Why cannot she under-*

*stand about boats.* 'I'm out of here.' *You're a cad.* 'I'm a hard man.' *No good will come of this.* 'Oh yeah.' *You're a selfish fool. An idiot. No hoper. Pathetic. Dumb. Stupid.* 'The voyage goes on.'

It was Saturday. Micaela was gone. Off I went to the Captainery and asked what the weather forecast looked like for the next few days. There were no great warnings or anything serious on the horizon. The officer said with a Gallic shrug, 'Nothing bad.' So I decided to go. I went up town. It was a busy rush hour shopping scene. I bought myself a cooked roast chicken, returned to the harbour, cast off the shore lines and motored out of Sete.

The weather indeed was fine as *Molly B* headed out into the Gulf of Leon. Blue sea, blue sky. I motor sailed for about five hours and then sailed all night under genoa and mizzen. By the following midday I was over 100 miles south of Sete. The sky went grey and the wind increased all afternoon. By that evening, as the sun went down, I dropped the mizzen and lay hove to under storm jib. I was confident that *Molly B* would look after herself as she had done many times

before. I was attempting to maintain position between Menorca and Sardinia. I slept easily that night as the storm raged outside.

Early the following morning light was just breaking. I think I was awake, lying in my bunk on the lee side. There was an almighty whoosh and then a BANG as *Molly B* was forced up in the air and then flipped head over heels. A complete 360 degree flip and probably stern over bow. I suppose it could have been a so called rogue wave if such things exist. There was a terrible mess in the cabin. I had not been expecting trouble and no proper stowage had been done. It was a bit like being inside a tumble dryer with all the contents of the boat. Luckily a heavy anchor and chain was stowed well forward. *Molly B* came upright. There was a lot of water in the bilge, up above the floor boards. This water mixed with everything including a horrible mess of ash from the stove.

I rushed on deck. The two masts were gone, hanging over the side in the water. The main boom and gaff, stowed on the gallows, had been split in two and all crushed into the dinghy which was crushed like an egg shell. I threw the remains overboard. The life raft

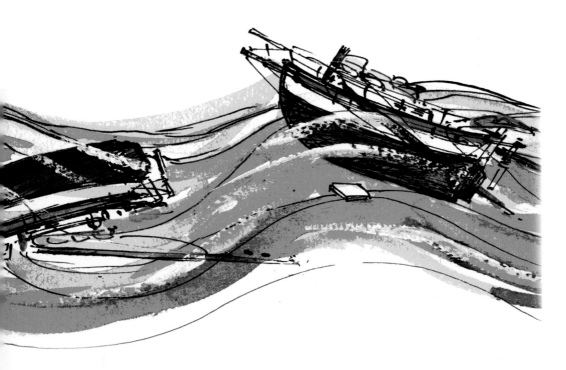

which was stowed under the dinghy was intact. The bubble dome over the chart table was smashed. The forward hatch was gone. It had not been locked from below. This proved to be a big loss. The remains of the masts were hanging over the side in a mess of rigging. The lifelines and pushpits were all bent and broken. I could not find the bilge pump handle. It must have gone overboard. *Molly B* has obviously been lifted up and slammed down with great force on to the sea in a sort of an upside down belly flop or pitch pole.

Down below, in the cabin, at first I think that *Molly B* is taking water. It's difficult to establish if the level has stabilised as the water sloshes about. There are gurgling sounds which are worrying. The stump of the main mast is out of its step and against the hull. Perhaps it has holed the boat. At first I panic and think that with no bilge pump I will have to abandon ship. I have two EPIRBs (emergency radio beacons). I manage to find one of them and activate it. There is a terrible mess. Food, crockery, tins, books, clothes, tools everywhere. I had not closed the latches on the lockers or drawers. I try and improvise a bilge pump handle but it is not successful. Then I start using a bucket. I hoist the water up out the companionway and over the side. Then I discover that using the bucket and emptying it into the galley sink is faster. The level starts to drop. I breathe a sigh of relief.

Getting the water level under control takes most of the day. I am very sick and weak. I bail for a while then I retch, trying to vomit. Then I lie down for a bit then I start bailing again. This goes on as a pattern for the whole day. I had no energy to do much about the mast and sails and rigging wreckage. The masts bang against the hull and the rigging saws at the gunnel and the lifelines. But I have confidence in the thick hull.

*Molly B* spends that night lying ahull. The GPS, the VHF and Nav lights are gone but I am optimistic. I manage to haul some of the mast wreckage on to the deck and some of the mizzen wreckage I tie alongside. I am anxious to save the brand new rigging. I should

simply have cut it away. In the afternoon of this second day (Tuesday) I get the motor going and motor to the north for a bit. I am confident that I can make port under motor and even start thinking of ways to set a jury rig. I get the paraffin stove working and have tea and biscuits. About dusk on that day a large ship passes close by.

A tanker. I do not try and signal though I do try and talk to them on a hand held VHF which I have. There is no response and I am not sure the VHF is working. I am not that worried. I am confident of making some port under motor.

Again I lay ahull overnight. It is Wednesday. The wind is strong and the sea choppy but nothing *Molly B* cannot take. I attempt to plug the fore hatch by making a frame out of four pieces of wood and covering them with a sail bag. I put it in place in the hatch like a mosquito net. It turns out to be totally inadequate. I was reluctant to drive any nails or screws into the deck of *Molly B*. This shows how confident I was that things would be OK. It also shows how badly I misjudged the situation I was in.

That night, Wednesday night, there was an intense thunder storm and disturbance. This was followed by very heavy northerly winds. By the morning the wind has built up to storm force 10. The sea was a mess of spindrift as the top is blown off the waves. As

the sea builds up *Molly B* starts to take a beating. I consider running before the wind. But I am so unsure of *Molly B*'s position now that I fear we might be near Sardinia. Also I do not think I can stay on the helm long enough to ride out the storm.

By now the waves are breaking over *Molly B* at regular intervals as she lays ahull, broadside on to the sea. Every now and then as a particularly big wave breaks at the wrong time in the wrong place, *Molly B* takes a real pasting, almost a knock down. I decide to try to rig some sort of a sea anchor to keep the bow pointing into the sea. I stream the actual anchor off the bow hoping its drag will be enough to keep the bow into the waves. It seems to work for most of the afternoon. It's a huge effort for me to do anything.

I noticed that the barometer was moving rapidly up. I wrongly assumed that this might be good news and an indication that the front had passed. But in fact the wind continued to increase and the seas continued to build up. The mess of rigging and heavy broken spars all over the deck became a huge problem. I should have dumped the lot. Now it was too late. Every time *Molly B* would take a big hit, the mass of heavy equipment would fly from side to side. Because of the cat's cradle of rigging I could not dump it. The cover which I had built for the fore hatch gets blown away like an autumn leaf. The water is now able to enter the cabin from the fore hatch, the main mast hole in the deck, the broken dome over the chart table and a bit through the seat lockers. The sea is playing with me like the Old Man of the Sea in Hemmingway's great story. In this version the sea wins.

Around dusk with the storm at its height, *Molly B* was hit by another huge wave. I was down below and crushed in a mess of cushions, gear and debris. I struggled to free myself. The boat had stabilised upside down. I stood on the ceiling of the cabin and calmly surveyed the situation. There was a lot of water in the hull. I could feel the pressure building up against my ears. Maybe the boat was sinking into the depths. I went aft and looked at the closed companionway at my feet. It did not look easy to open it and swim out. I went forward to the open fore hatch. I could see clear blue water at my feet and thought of diving in and getting out of the hull. But I said to myself, 'Wait, she must right herself.' There were three tons of lead ballast up there above my head. So I waited standing above the escape route at my feet. It might have been two minutes. I could hear the roaring of the waves. I could feel the pressure in my ears as the water filled the hull. A big wave hit *Molly B* again and over she went, righting herself.

There was a lot of water in the hull. Much more than there had been the first time *Molly B* had flipped 360 degrees. It was above the level of the bunks in the cabin. I started bailing into the sink as I had before and the water level starts to fall. I start throwing things overboard in desperation as I should have done when I had the chance. The batteries short out in a cloud of smoke. I check on deck. It's a grim sight. I check to see if I still have the life raft. I go below. Another big wave crashes over and *Molly B* does another roll through 360 degrees. I am under water in a mess of loose equipment and struggle to release myself. There is even more water in the boat this time. I notice that the water is coming in through the galley sink rather than draining out. I realise it is the end. If she rolls another time I am unlikely to survive in the cabin. If she rolls another time while I am on deck I am also going to be injured and drowned. *Molly B* is sinking and there is nothing I can do about it.

I grabbed a brief case with some papers, some cheese and a bottle of Coke. I put on a life jacket. I threw the life raft into the water and it inflated. I walked up to the bow where it sits against the hull. I stepped carefully into it and cut the line attaching the raft to *Molly B*. I did not want the rogue hull to sink the life raft. The raft drifts off down wind. I see *Molly B* settling low in the water. The life raft drifts further away in the fading light. That was the last I saw of *Molly B*.

*Molly B* was gone. Forever. To the bottom of the sea. My obsession for the last quarter of a century had been to have my own boat, a boat which could go anywhere. Now it was gone, finished, over. I had worked, sweated, saved, struggled, done without, taken risks, just to have my dream boat. It had brought me great joy, pride, adventures, freedom, learning, and a place to call home. Now it was gone. My time in Vancouver, building *Molly B*, had been the happiest and most carefree of my life. Sailing *Molly B*, engineless, through the Panama Canal from Vancouver to Ireland had been a voyage, an achievement of which I was proud. Sailing *Molly B* around the world had brought me to Micaela and around Cape Horn. All that was now buried under a mile or so of stormy, cold, Mediterranean water.

I hardly had time to reflect on these niceties as I lay spread-eagled in a big puddle on the floor of the bucking life raft. I was wet through, shivering, in the dark, the waves crashing all round, and things looked grim. I was like a character in a Greek odyssey who has offended the Gods. What more could the sea do to me? Was this the end?

# Chapter 17

# 'A Thousand Thousand Slimy Things'

*'And a thousand thousand slimy things*
*Lived on; and so did I.'*

It was getting dark when I got into the life raft. It is an Avon four person life raft, the smallest one available. It measures about five feet in diameter with a tent like canopy over the top. It has an inflatable floor which is important for insulation. The rate of drift is limited by a small sea anchor, like an underwater parachute. This also holds the raft with the entrance facing away from the wind. All things considered and in retrospect, the raft is set up very well and did what it was supposed to do. I suppose it must be the best investment I ever made. I have met people who threw the life raft into the water and it did not inflate!

There is a small light in the raft under the canopy. The motion is still very violent and I slide about on the rubber floor. There is a set of instructions there in front of me. I figure out how to inflate the floor of the raft with the pump provided. This improves my situation as water lying in the bottom of the raft now drains to the side and has less of a tendency to wet me. It also provides insulation from the cold seawater outside. I find a bailer but it is difficult to use as it re-

quires two hands in a sort of a scoop like action. One hand is needed to hang on to the side of the raft in the violent motion. It is like being in the surf on a beach.

There is a triangular opening in the canopy which has a clever Velcro seal. This works quite well, especially when I figure out how to close it carefully so that it is as strong as possible. When a big wave smashes against it, it can force open the Velcro and flood the raft. Water also gets in through a small port type vent which faces the wind. I did not learn that this vent can be sealed so took a lot of water through it.

I figured out a better bailer for getting rid of the water which gets into the raft and which slops around on the floor. There is a knife in the raft. I cut the top off the coke bottle and use the bottom half to bail out the water from the 'gutters' at the side of the raft.

I settle in for the night as the wind howls and the waves break all round. I lay spread-eagled on my back in the bottom of the raft, trying to keep the centre of gravity as low as possible. I am lying in a pool of water which I have to bail out every ten minutes or so. I am soaked to the skin and have been for the last two uncontrollable days. I shiver. I eat a small bite of cheese every now and then thinking this might help.

I became obsessed by time and looking at my watch. Time seems to move very slowly. I say that if I can get through five minutes I can get through 10 minutes. If I can get through 10 minutes then I can get through 20 minutes. And so on. Every half hour or so I have to bail out the water on the floor of the raft as it is uncomfortable to lie in. The bailing is a relief from the cold and the stiffness.

I have time to calmly think about my situation. It does not look good. If I do not drown surely the cold will get me. The cold seems like the most likely. There is nothing I can do except lie there.

The waves roar by, sometimes with the impact of an express train. 'That was a big one,' I say. The raft shudders with the impact. I lie in the pool of water on the floor and shiver uncontrollably. My teeth rattle against each other. I cannot stop them. How long can I last? I get to midnight. There is no sign of the wind easing.

It was now Friday. *Molly B* had had her first roll and dismasting the previous Monday. I had been in the same set of wet clothes and wet weather gear since then. I was exhausted. I was lying on the floor of the life raft trying to think myself warm. The wind seems to change direction a bit. This increases the problem as the wind now blows across the seas which have built up. Suddenly there is an almighty whoosh and a huge wave capsizes the raft. I am under water and wrapped in a tent.

The roof of the life raft was held up by an inflated tube. This whole canopy collapsed in on top of me with the pressure of the water. I hold my breath. I push and shove and scrape against the fabric of the canopy. I find the exit. I pull at the Velcro. I rip the opening open and swim out. I am caught in some lines. Still holding my breath I free myself. I swim to the surface. My head pops out and I cling to the side of the upturned raft. I regain my breath. What now. The water is cold, the waves breaking around in the darkness. I manage to climb on top of the raft using some hand grips. It is quite an effort. I realise what I must do to right the raft, having read the instructions. I find the handle on the underside of the raft and manage to point it in the direction of the wind. I pull up on the handle. The raft rises, the wind catches the underside and over the raft goes. It is floating upright. I am in the water again, clinging on to the side of the raft.

I clamber in the entrance. The raft is half full of water. All of the contents not tied on are gone. I have lost my bag with papers, my sea boots which I had taken off and the coke can bailer. I manage to bail out with a large plastic bag which is part of the life raft kit, and a sponge.

I sat there thinking, 'this looks bad'. If we were to flip again I do not know if I would have had the strength to repeat that performance. I worry what will happen to my body, will it get eaten by sharks. Will it wash up on the beaches of Libya? I pray. If I get out of this I will be good forevermore. I will make a pilgrimage to Lough Derg like my dear Mum used to do. My whole life seems to drift before me, like they say it does. It looks like the end.

Dawn breaks slowly. The wind dies down but the seas still remain confused and dangerous. A weak sun comes out. Things improve. I start to warm up. I try and make the raft more comfortable.

I can open the entrance and scan the horizon. Almost on schedule, at midday, I spy a ship on the horizon. It is heading my way. I wave. I get a flare ready. I try to imagine a man on the bridge of the ship keeping watch – the eyes of the ship. I fire the flare, possibly a bit too soon. It arches up into the air and descends on its parachute. Nothing happens. The ship marches on. I let off a smoke flare as the ship appears to be the closest it is going to be. This is a hand-held flare which lets off a big cloud of dense smoke. Still the ship marches on. No indication that they have seen me. I wave but do not want to let off any more of the two flares I have left. Now the stern of the ship is heading for the horizon. They did not see me. Suddenly, it changes course. It is turning. It is definitely turning; they are coming back for me. I get very emotional.

The *MV Concordia* makes one pass of the life raft but it is not near enough to throw a line to me. The captain shouts from the bridge, 'I go around again.' And so they do. This time they are closer and heave me a line telling me to attach it to the raft. The raft swings in to the side of the ship on this line. A long ladder comes down the side. I am able to climb up under my own steam. Two men, one on either side bring me to the galley of the ship. There are smiling Filipino faces everywhere. I am quite emotional. I can only repeat over and over. 'You saved me. You saved me.'

# Afterword

*The MV Concordia* was a large bulk carrier on route from the Baltic to Sardinia. The captain was an East German. He kept telling me that 'I now have two chances at heaven'. Meaning that this was the second time his ship had picked up a castaway. The crew was all Filipino and the mate, one Jeasu Balabosa, had been on watch and seen my flares. They handed me over to the ship's agents in Oritsano, Sardinia and three days later I was on my way back to Dublin.

*Molly B* sank in over 2,000 metres depth of water. I have often wondered if some diver might come upon it and raise the wreck. At that depth and as time marches on there is very little likelihood of that happening.

I eventually reconciled with Micaela. We are married now and have two children. I still think that it is fortunate that Micaela was not on board *Molly B* on that fateful last trip.

My Dad died shortly before *Molly B* set out on her last trip.

There is a large and revered literature connected with the Tahiti ketch. Many voyages of note are recorded. Notable among them Jean Gau and Tom Steele. People are still building Tahiti ketches and there is at least one production version. But they remain slow boats and that's an understatement.